The **M**inimal **E**nglish **T**est

音声ダウンロード

牧　秀樹
張　　超

大学入学共通テスト**聴解版**

最小英語テスト （MET） ドリル

大学入学
共通テスト
聴解版

開拓社

まえがき

　「大学入学共通テスト英語の聴解問題に**慣れておきたい。**」そんな方に，このドリルをお勧めします。『**最小英語テスト（MET）ドリル**』の**第6弾**です。高校生，大学生，社会人，そして，英語からしばらく遠ざかっている方にも楽しんでいただけます。

　音声を使って，1回3分から4分程度で終わる問題が，大学入学共通テスト第1回（2021年1月）から第3回（2023年1月）までの過去3年間に渡る英語聴解問題に基づいて作成され，合計30題収載されています。このドリルにある簡易テストは，最小英語テスト（The Minimal English Test＝MET）と呼びます。時間が最短の英語テストだからです。METについてのより詳しい説明は，牧秀樹著『The Minimal English Test（最小英語テスト）研究』（2018年，開拓社）を参考にしてください。

　それよりも，早く音声を聞いて，練習問題をやっていただければ，METがどんなものか実感できると思います。このドリルが，みなさんの心の友となってくれるといいなと願っています。

　本ドリルを作成するに当たっては，大学入学共通テスト英語2021-2023年聴解問題（本試験と追試験）の英文とその音声を利用しています。英文と音声の使用を許可してくださった大学入試センターに心より感謝いたします。また，困難な時世の中，本書の出版を引き受けてくださった開拓社の川田賢氏にも深く感謝いたします。

2024年1月　　牧 秀樹・張 超

目　次

MET のやり方

　MET は，英語の音声を聞きながら，単語を埋めるだけの簡単なテストです。音声だけを聞いていれば，それほど速いとは感じませんが，いったんテストが始まると，突然，襲い掛かるように速く感じます。ですから，単語が，聞きとれなかったり，書ききれなかったりした場合は，あきらめて，すぐに，次の空所に移るようにしてください。そうしないと，一度に5つくらい空所が吹っ飛んでしまうことがあり，得点の低下につながってしまいます。

　1題終わるごとに，次のページに日本語訳と解答があるので，答え合わせをしながら，書ききれなかった箇所を確認し，また，意味が分からなかった箇所も，同時に確認してください。日本語訳は，なるべく理解しやすいように，あえて，英文を前から訳しています。英語母語話者は，実際この順番で文の意味を理解していますので，わざわざ，英文で最初の方に現れる動詞を，長い日本文の最後に置かないようにしています。

　本試験15題と追試験15題があります。追試験の方が若干難度が高くなっています。また，各15題は，5題ずつ3つのグループに分かれ，3つのグループは，進むにつれ，難度が上がっています。15題行って，どれだけ自分が伸びたかを測定するには，第1題目の MET を複写しておいて，その第1題目の MET だけは採点せず（つまり，答えを見ず），他の14題が終わってから，その複写した第1題目の MET を行い，そこで，第1題目の MET を2枚，同時に採点してください。何点伸びたかがはっきり分かります。

　それでは，どうぞ，MET で豊かな時間を。共通テストの心の友。

第1章

大学入学共通テスト本試験版
MET 問題

　この章には，問題が，15題あります。全問題は，大学入学共通テスト英語本試験の聞き取りテストの過去問題の音声と英文を基に作られているので，MET 2021 本 (1) のように，名前が付けられています。各問題には，空所（　）があります。音声を聞きながら，（　）の中に，英単語を入れてください。15題は，5題ずつ3つのグループに分かれ，3つのグループは，進むにつれ，難度が上がっています。

　1題終わるごとに，答え合わせをすることができます。各問題の次のページには，その英文の日本語訳が，そして，その次のページには，解答が太字で示されています。答え合わせが終わったら，問題のページに戻り，点数を記入しておくことができます。

　まずは，次のページにある練習問題から始めてみましょう。どんな作業をするかわかります。

音声 Track **00**

MET 練習問題

／5点

英語の音声を聞きながら，（　　）の中に，英単語を入れてください。

We're almost at the top of the mountain.　Whew!　I hope there's a nice （　　　　）[1].　There's a view of the valley and a small lake.　It's beautiful. Great!　I want （　　　　）[2] get a good picture.　It's such a nice morning. I'm sure the view （　　　　）[3] be clear.　Ah, here we are.　Oh, no!　Where's the valley?　There's too much fog.　We can't （　　　　）[4] anything.　Well, let's have some lunch first.　Maybe the fog will clear later.　OK.　Let's do that.　What did （　　　　）[5] bring for lunch?　Oh, I thought you brought our lunch.

MET 練習問題 日本語訳

問題英文の日本語訳を確認しよう。

もうすぐ山頂だね。ふぅ！ いい景色が見られるといいね。谷と小さな湖が見える。きれいだ。いいねえ！ いい写真が撮りたいな。素敵な朝だ。きっと視界が晴れるよ。さあ，着いた。あれまあ！ 谷はどこだろう？ 霧が多すぎ。何も見えないな。じゃあ，先にお昼にしよう。霧はそのうち晴れるよ。そうだね。そうしよう。昼食に何を持ってきたの？ あら，私たちのお弁当も持ってきてくれてるって思ってた。

MET 練習問題 解答

解答付き英文を見ながら，英語の音声をもう一度聞いてみよう。

We're almost at the top of the mountain. Whew! I hope there's a nice (**view**)[1]. There's a view of the valley and a small lake. It's beautiful. Great! I want (**to**)[2] get a good picture. It's such a nice morning. I'm sure the view (**will**)[3] be clear. Ah, here we are. Oh, no! Where's the valley? There's too much fog. We can't (**see**)[4] anything. Well, let's have some lunch first. Maybe the fog will clear later. OK. Let's do that. What did (**you**)[5] bring for lunch? Oh, I thought you brought our lunch.

MET 2021 本 (1)

英語の音声を聞きながら，（　）の中に，英単語を入れてください。

Can I have some more juice? I'm still thirsty. Where can (   )¹ go this weekend? Ah, I know. How about Sunset Beach? To start working (   )² Hiroshima next week, Yuji moved from Chiba the day after graduation. I won't (   )³ David any more ice cream today. I gave him (   )⁴ after lunch. Almost everyone at the bus stop is wearing a (   )⁵. Nancy already has a lot of striped T-shirts and animal T-shirts. Now she's buying another design. (   )⁶ girl's mother is painting a picture of herself. Maria, let me get (   )⁷ water bottle. OK, mine has a cup on the (   )⁸. Does it have a big handle on (   )⁹ side? No, but it has a strap. Which water bottle is Maria's? (   )¹⁰ about this animal one? It's cute, but robots should be able to (   )¹¹ more. That's right. Like the one that can clean the house. Exactly. That's (   )¹² best. Which robot will the man most likely vote (   )¹³? Don't you need garbage bags? No, they'll be provided. But maybe I'll need these. Right, (   )¹⁴ could get pretty dirty. And it's sunny today, so I should take this, (   )¹⁵. What will the daughter take? Excuse me, where's the elevator? (   )¹⁶ there, next to the lockers across from the restrooms. Is (   )¹⁷ all the way at the end? That's right, (   )¹⁸ before the stairs. Where is the elevator?

MET 2021 本（1）日本語訳

問題英文の日本語訳を確認しよう。

ジュースをもう少しいただけますか？ まだ喉が渇いているので。今週末はどこに行こうか？ ああ，そうね。サンセットビーチはどう？ 来週から広島で働き始めるので，ユウジは卒業の翌日に千葉から引っ越してきた。今日はもうデイビッドにアイスクリームをあげない。昼食後に少しあげたんだから。バス停にいるほとんどの人が帽子をかぶってる。ナンシーはすでに縞のTシャツや動物Tシャツをたくさん持ってる。今，別のデザインのを買おうとしてる。その女の子の母親は自分の絵を描いている。マリア，水筒を取りますよ。ありがとう，私のは上にカップが付いてる。横に大きな手が付いてる？ 付いてないよ，でもストラップは付いてる。マリアの水筒はどれですか？ この動物のはどう？ それはかわいいけど，ロボットにはもっとできるんじゃないかな。そうだね。家が掃除できる人みたいに。その通り。それが一番だ。この男性は結局どのロボットに投票するかな？ ゴミ袋は要らないの？ 要らないよ，だってもらえるから。でも，ひょっとしたらこれ必要になるかも。そうだね，けっこう汚れるかもね。あげくに今日は晴れたから，これも持っていこうかな。この娘は何を持っているでしょう？ すみません，エレベーターはどこですか？ そこをもうちょっと行ったところ，ロッカーの隣，トイレの向かい側の。ここを最後までずっと行きますか？ そう，階段の手前まで。エレベーターはどこにありますか？

MET 2021 本 (1) 解答

解答付き英文を見ながら，英語の音声をもう一度聞いてみよう。

Can I have some more juice? I'm still thirsty. Where can (**we**)¹ go this weekend? Ah, I know. How about Sunset Beach? To start working (**in**)² Hiroshima next week, Yuji moved from Chiba the day after graduation. I won't (**give**)³ David any more ice cream today. I gave him (**some**)⁴ after lunch. Almost everyone at the bus stop is wearing a (**hat**)⁵. Nancy already has a lot of striped T-shirts and animal T-shirts. Now she's buying another design. (**The**)⁶ girl's mother is painting a picture of herself. Maria, let me get (**your**)⁷ water bottle. OK, mine has a cup on the (**top**)⁸. Does it have a big handle on (**the**)⁹ side? No, but it has a strap. Which water bottle is Maria's? (**What**)¹⁰ about this animal one? It's cute, but robots should be able to (**do**)¹¹ more. That's right. Like the one that can clean the house. Exactly. That's (**the**)¹² best. Which robot will the man most likely vote (**for**)¹³? Don't you need garbage bags? No, they'll be provided. But maybe I'll need these. Right, (**you**)¹⁴ could get pretty dirty. And it's sunny today, so I should take this, (**too**)¹⁵. What will the daughter take? Excuse me, where's the elevator? (**Down**)¹⁶ there, next to the lockers across from the restrooms. Is (**it**)¹⁷ all the way at the end? That's right, (**just**)¹⁸ before the stairs. Where is the elevator?

MET 2021 本 (2)

Hello, Tina. What are you doing these days? Hi, Mr. Corby. I'm busy rehearsing for (　　　　)^1 musical. Really? When's the performance? It's April 14th, at three. Please come! I'd love to! Oh... no, wait. There's (　　　　)^2 teachers' meeting that day, and I can't miss it. (　　　　)^3 good luck! Thanks. Where (　　　　)^4 these boxes go? Put them (　　　　)^5 the shelf, in the back, and then (　　　　)^6 the cans in front of them, because we'll use (　　　　)^7 cans first. How about these bags of flour and sugar? Oh, just leave (　　　　)^8 on the counter. I'll put them in the containers later. (　　　　)^9 didn't know the meeting was canceled. Why didn't you tell (　　　　)^{10}? Didn't you see my email? No. Did you send (　　　　)^{11} one? I sure did. Can you check again? Just (　　　　)^{12} minute.... Um... there's definitely no email from you. Uh-oh, I must have (　　　　)^{13} it to the wrong person. I've decided to visit you next March. Great! That's (　　　　)^{14} good time. The weather should be much warmer by (　　　　)^{15}. That's good to hear. I hope it's not (　　　　)^{16} early for the cherry blossoms. Well, you never know exactly when they (　　　　)^{17} bloom, but the weather will be nice. Hey, did (　　　　)^{18} get a ticket for tomorrow's baseball game? Don't ask! Oh no! You didn't? (　　　　)^{19} happened? Well... when I tried to buy one yesterday, they were already (　　　　)^{20} out. I knew I should've tried to get (　　　　)^{21} earlier. I see. Now I understand why you're upset. Look! That's (　　　　)^{21} famous actor—the one who played the prime minister in that film (　　　　)^{23} year. Hmm, I can't remember his name. You mean Kenneth Miller? Yes! Isn't (　　　　)^{24} him over there? I don't think so. Kenneth Miller would look a little older. Oh, you're right. That's (　　　　)^{25} him.

MET 2021 (2) 日本語訳

問題英文の日本語訳を確認しよう。

ティナ，こんにちは。最近何してる？ コービーさん，こんにちは。忙しくしてますよ，ミュージカルのリハーサルで。本当に？ 公演はいつ？ 4月14日の3時。来て下さいね！ もちろん！ あれ，ちょっと待って。その日は職員会議があるなあ。ちょっとさぼれないな。でも応援してますよ！ ありがとう。これらの箱はどこに置くの？ 後ろの棚に置いて，缶をその前に置いて。缶を最初に使用するから。小麦粉と砂糖の入った袋は？ ああ，カウンターの上に置いておいて。後で容器に入れるから。知らなかったよ，会議がキャンセルされたなんて。なんで教えてくれなかったの？ 私のメールを見なかったの？ ええ？ 私に送ってくれた？ もちろん。もう一度確認してみて？ ちょっと待って，あれ，メールないよ。ああ，違う人に送っちゃったみたいだ。来年の3月にあなたを訪れることにしたよ。素晴らしい！ 良い時期。その頃にはもっと暖かくなるはずだ。よかった。桜に早すぎないといいんだけど。そうだね，正確にいつ咲くかはわからないけど，天気は良いと思うよ。ねえ，明日の野球の試合のチケット，買った？ 聞かないでよ！ なんてこった！ 買わなかったの？ どうしたんだよ？ なんというか，昨日買おうとしたらもう売り切れだったんだ。分かってたんだよ，もっと早く買うべきだって。なるほど。だから動揺してんだね。見て！ あれ，有名な俳優よ。昨年あの映画で首相を演じた人。うーん，名前が思い出せないなあ。ケネス・ミラーのこと？ そう！ あそこにいるのは彼じゃない？ そうは思わないなあ。ケネス・ミラーはもう少し老けて見えるじゃない？ ああ，そうだね。ありゃ，彼じゃないね。

MET 2021 本（2）解答

解答付き英文を見ながら，英語の音声をもう一度聞いてみよう。

Hello, Tina. What are you doing these days? Hi, Mr. Corby. I'm busy rehearsing for（ **a** ）[1] musical. Really? When's the performance? It's April 14th, at three. Please come! I'd love to! Oh... no, wait. There's（ **a** ）[2] teachers' meeting that day, and I can't miss it. （ **But** ）[3] good luck! Thanks. Where（ **do** ）[4] these boxes go? Put them（ **on** ）[5] the shelf, in the back, and then（ **put** ）[6] the cans in front of them, because we'll use（ **the** ）[7] cans first. How about these bags of flour and sugar? Oh, just leave（ **them** ）[8] on the counter. I'll put them in the containers later. （ **I** ）[9] didn't know the meeting was canceled. Why didn't you tell（ **me** ）[10]? Didn't you see my email? No. Did you send（ **me** ）[11] one? I sure did. Can you check again? Just（ **a** ）[12] minute.... Um... there's definitely no email from you. Uh-oh, I must have（ **sent** ）[13] it to the wrong person. I've decided to visit you next March. Great! That's（ **a** ）[14] good time. The weather should be much warmer by （ **then** ）[15]. That's good to hear. I hope it's not（ **too** ）[16] early for the cherry blossoms. Well, you never know exactly when they（ **will** ）[17] bloom, but the weather will be nice. Hey, did（ **you** ）[18] get a ticket for tomorrow's baseball game? Don't ask! Oh no! You didn't? （ **What** ）[19] happened? Well... when I tried to buy one yesterday, they were already（ **sold** ）[20] out. I knew I should've tried to get（ **it** ）[21] earlier. I see. Now I understand why you're upset. Look! That's（ **the** ）[22] famous actor—the one who played the prime minister in that film（ **last** ）[23] year. Hmm, I can't remember his name. You mean Kenneth Miller? Yes! Isn't（ **that** ）[24] him over there? I don't think so. Kenneth Miller would look a little older. Oh, you're right. That's（ **not** ）[25] him.

英語の音声を聞きながら，（　　）の中に，英単語を入れてください。

One hundred university students were asked this question: How do you spend most (　　　　)[1] your time outside of school? They were asked to select (　　　　)[2] one item from five choices: "going out with friends," "playing online games," "studying," "working part-time," and "other." The (　　　　)[3] popular selection was "going out with friends," with 30 percent choosing this category. Exactly half (　　　　)[4] percentage of students selected "working part-time." "playing online games" received a quarter of all the votes. The third (　　　　)[5] selected category was "studying," which came after "playing online games." We've discounted some DVD titles. Basically, the discount rate depends on their release (　　　　)[6]. The price of any title released in the year 2000 (　　　　)[7] before is reduced 30%. Titles that were released between 2001 and 2010 are 20% off. Anything released (　　　　)[8] recently than that isn't discounted. Oh, there's one more thing! The titles with a (　　　　)[9] are only 10% off, regardless of their release date, because they (　　　　)[10] popular.

I love *It's Really Funny You Should Say That!* I don't know why it's not higher (　　　　)[11] the rankings. I've seen a lot of musicals, but (　　　　)[12] of them beats this one. It's pretty serious, but it does (　　　　)[13] one really funny part. It's performed only on weekdays. You'll enjoy *My Darling, Don't Make Me Laugh.* I laughed the whole time. It's (　　　　)[14] been running for a month but already has very (　　　　)[15] ticket sales. Actually, that's why they started performing it on weekends, too. If ( )[16] like comedies, I recommend *Sam and Keith's Laugh Out Loud Adventure*. My friend said it was ( )[17] good. I've seen some good reviews about it, too, ( )[18] plan carefully because it's only on at the weekend. Since you're visiting New York, don't miss *You Put the 'Fun' in Funny*. It's ( )[19] romance with a few comedy scenes. For some reason, it hasn't ( )[20] very good ticket sales. It's staged every day of the week.

MET 2021（3）日本語訳

問題英文の日本語訳を確認しよう。

100 人の大学生に次の質問をした。学校以外の時間のほとんどをどのように過ごしますか？ 次の5 つの選択肢から 1 つだけ選んでもらった。「友達と出かける」「オンラインゲームをする」「勉強する」「アルバイトをする」最も多かった回答は「友達と出かける」で，30% がこれを選択した。ちょうどその半数の学生が「アルバイトをする」を選択した。「オンラインゲームをする」は全体の 4 分の 1 だった。3 位は「勉強する」で，その一つ前が，「オンラインゲームをする」だった。一部の DVD 商品を値下げした。基本的に割引率は，発売日によって異なる。2000 年以前に発売された商品はすべて 30% 値下げされる。2001 年から 2010 年までに発売された商品は 20% オフ。それより後に発売されたものは割引されない。ああ，もう 1 つ！ 星印の商品は人気商品のため，発売日にかかわらず 10%OFF。

私は，「It's Really Funny You Should Say That!」が大好き。なぜもっと上位に来ないのか分からない。ミュージカルをたくさん見てきましたが，これに勝るものはない。かなりまじめな内容だけど，本当におもしろい部分が 1 つある。平日のみ上演。「My Darling, Don't Make me Laugh」が楽しめるよ。私はずっと笑ってた。上演されてまだ 1 か月だけど，チケットの売れ行きはすでに相当高くなってる。実は，そんなわけで週末にも上演されることになったの。コメディーが好きなら，「Sam and Keith's Laugh Out Loud Adventure」を勧めますよ。友人はとても良かったと言ってます。良い評価もいくつか見かけたけど，行くなら，慎重に計画を立てて。上演は，週末だけなので。ニューヨークを訪れるんだから，「You Put the 'Fun' in Funny」は，見逃せないよ。ロマンスなんだけど，コメディシーンもいくつかある。どういうわけか，チケットの売れ行きはあまりよくない。毎日上演されてる。

MET 2021 本 (3) 解答

解答付き英文を見ながら，英語の音声をもう一度聞いてみよう。

One hundred university students were asked this question: How do you spend most (**of**)[1] your time outside of school? They were asked to select (**only**)[2] one item from five choices: "going out with friends," "playing online games," "studying," "working part-time," and "other." The (**most**)[3] popular selection was "going out with friends," with 30 percent choosing this category. Exactly half (**that**)[4] percentage of students selected "working part-time." "playing online games" received a quarter of all the votes. The third (**most**)[5] selected category was "studying," which came after "playing online games." We've discounted some DVD titles. Basically, the discount rate depends on their release (**date**)[6]. The price of any title released in the year 2000 (**and**)[7] before is reduced 30%. Titles that were released between 2001 and 2010 are 20% off. Anything released (**more**)[8] recently than that isn't discounted. Oh, there's one more thing! The titles with a (**star**)[9] are only 10% off, regardless of their release date, because they (**are**)[10] popular.

I love *It's Really Funny You Should Say That!* I don't know why it's not higher (**in**)[11] the rankings. I've seen a lot of musicals, but (**none**)[12] of them beats this one. It's pretty serious, but it does (**have**)[13] one really funny part. It's performed only on weekdays. You'll enjoy *My Darling, Don't Make Me Laugh.* I laughed the whole time. It's (**only**)[14] been running for a month but already has very (**high**)[15] ticket sales. Actually, that's why they started performing it on weekends, too. If (**you**)[16] like comedies, I recommend *Sam and Keith's Laugh Out Loud Adventure.* My friend said it was (**very**)[17] good. I've seen some good reviews about it, too, (**but**)[18] plan carefully because it's only on at the weekend. Since you're visiting New York, don't miss *You Put the 'Fun' in Funny.* It's (**a**)[19] romance with a few comedy scenes. For some reason, it hasn't (**had**)[20] very good ticket sales. It's staged every day of the week.

MET 2021 本 (4)

英語の音声を聞きながら，（　　）の中に，英単語を入れてください。

What is happiness? Can we be happy and promote sustainable development? Since 2012, (　　　　　)[1] *World Happiness Report* has been issued by a United Nations organization to develop new approaches (　　　　)[2] economic sustainability for the sake of happiness and well-being. The reports (　　　　)[3] that Scandinavian countries are consistently ranked as the happiest societies on earth. But (　　　　)[4] makes them so happy? In Denmark, for example, leisure time is often spent (　　　)[5] others. That kind of environment makes Danish people happy thanks to a tradition called "hygge," spelled H-Y-G-G-E. Hygge means coziness or comfort (　　　)[6] describes the feeling of being loved. This word became well-known worldwide in 2016 as (　　　　)[7] interpretation of mindfulness or wellness. Now, hygge is at risk (　　　)[8] being commercialized. But hygge is not about the material things we see (　　　)[9] popular images like candlelit rooms and cozy bedrooms with hand-knit blankets. Real hygge happens anywhere—in public (　　　)[10] in private, indoors or outdoors, with or without candles. The main point (　　　)[11] hygge is to live a life connected with loved (　　　)[12] while making ordinary essential tasks meaningful and joyful. Perhaps Danish people are better at appreciating the small, "hygge" things in life because (　　　)[13] have no worries about basic necessities. Danish people willingly pay from 30 to 50 percent of their income (　　　)[14] tax. These high taxes pay for a good welfare system (　　　)[15] provides free healthcare and education. Once basic needs are met, more money doesn't guarantee (　　　)[16] happiness.

While money and material goods seem to be highly valued in some countries ( )[17] the US, people in Denmark place more value on socializing. Nevertheless, Denmark has above-average productivity according to ( )[18] OECD. Here's a graph based on OECD data. People in Denmark value private life over ( )[19], but it doesn't mean they produce less. The OECD found ( )[20] beyond a certain number of hours, working more overtime led to lower productivity. What ( )[21] you think?

MET 2021(4) 日本語訳

問題英文の日本語訳を確認しよう。

幸せって何でしょう？ 私たちは幸せのまま，持続可能な発展ができるでしょうか？ 2012 年以来，『世界幸福度報告書』が国連機関によって発行されています。それによって，経済的持続可能性のために新しいアプローチを探ります。それは，幸福と健康のためのものです。報告書によれば，スカンジナビア諸国は，一貫して，地球上で最も幸福な社会としてランク付けされています。しかし，何によって彼らはそんなに幸せを感じているんでしょうか？ 例えば，デンマークでは，よく，余暇を他の人と一緒に過ごします。このような環境によって，デンマークの人々は，幸せに感じています。それは，「ヒュッゲ」と呼ばれる，H-Y-G-G-E と綴られる，伝統のおかげです。ヒュッゲとは，心地よさや快適さを意味し，愛されているという感覚を表します。この言葉は，2016 年に世界中でよく知られるようになりました。マインドフルネスやウェルネスの解釈として。今，ヒュッゲは商品化の危機に直面しています。しかし，ヒュッゲは，一般的なイメージで見られる物質的なもののことではありません。キャンドルが灯る部屋とか，手編みの毛布がある居心地のいい寝床といった。本当のヒュッゲは，どこにでもあるものです。公共でもプライベートでも，屋内でも屋外でも，キャンドルのあるなしにかかわらず。ヒュッゲの大事なポイントは，愛する人たちとつながった生活を送ることです。日常の必要な作業を有意義で楽しいものにしながら。おそらくデンマーク人は，生活の中の小さな「ヒュッゲ」なものを評価することが上手なのです。基本的な必需品について心配することがないので。デンマーク人は所得の 30 〜 50 パーセントを喜んで税金として払います。これらの高い税金は，充実した福祉制度に支払われています。無料の医療と教育を提供する制度に。いったん基本的なニーズが満たされれば，より多くのお金がより多くの幸福を保証するわけではありません。金銭や物が高く評価される国もあるようですが，例えば，アメリカのような，デンマークの人々は社交性をより重視しています。それにもかかわらず，OECD によると，デンマークの生産性は，平均を上回っています。これは OECD のデータに基づいたグラフです。デンマークの人々は仕事よりもプライベートを大切にしますが，それは生産性が低いという意味ではありません。OECD は，次のことを発見しました。つまり，一定の時間を超えて，残業が増えると，生産性が低下するということです。どう思いますか？

MET 2021 本 (4) 解答

解答付き英文を見ながら，英語の音声をもう一度聞いてみよう。

What is happiness? Can we be happy and promote sustainable development? Since 2012, (**the**)[1] *World Happiness Report* has been issued by a United Nations organization to develop new approaches (**to**)[2] economic sustainability for the sake of happiness and well-being. The reports (**show**)[3] that Scandinavian countries are consistently ranked as the happiest societies on earth. But (**what**)[4] makes them so happy? In Denmark, for example, leisure time is often spent (**with**)[5] others. That kind of environment makes Danish people happy thanks to a tradition called "hygge," spelled H-Y-G-G-E. Hygge means coziness or comfort (**and**)[6] describes the feeling of being loved. This word became well-known worldwide in 2016 as (**an**)[7] interpretation of mindfulness or wellness. Now, hygge is at risk (**of**)[8] being commercialized. But hygge is not about the material things we see (**in**)[9] popular images like candlelit rooms and cozy bedrooms with hand-knit blankets. Real hygge happens anywhere—in public (**or**)[10] in private, indoors or outdoors, with or without candles. The main point (**of**)[11] hygge is to live a life connected with loved (**ones**)[12] while making ordinary essential tasks meaningful and joyful. Perhaps Danish people are better at appreciating the small, "hygge" things in life because (**they**)[13] have no worries about basic necessities. Danish people willingly pay from 30 to 50 percent of their income (**in**)[14] tax. These high taxes pay for a good welfare system (**that**)[15] provides free healthcare and education. Once basic needs are met, more money doesn't guarantee (**more**)[16] happiness. While money and material goods seem to be highly valued in some countries (**like**)[17] the US, people in Denmark place more value on socializing. Nevertheless, Denmark has above-average productivity according to (**the**)[18] OECD. Here's a graph based on OECD data. People in Denmark value private life over (**work**)[19], but it doesn't mean they produce less. The OECD found (**that**)[20] beyond a certain number of hours, working more overtime led to lower productivity. What (**do**)[21] you think?

MET 2021 本 (5)

英語の音声を聞きながら，（　　）の中に，英単語を入れてください。

Are you all right, Sho? What's wrong? Hey, Jane. It turns out a native French-speaking (　　　　)[1] family was not available... for my study abroad program in France. So (　　　　)[2] chose a host family instead of the dormitory, huh? Not yet. (　　　　)[3] was hoping for a native French-speaking family. Why? Well, I wanted to experience (　　　　)[4] spoken French. Sho, there are many varieties of French. I guess. But with (　　　　)[5] native French-speaking host family, I thought I could experience real language and real French culture. What's "real," anyway? France (　　　　)[6] diverse. Staying with a multilingual family could give you a genuine feel (　　　　)[7] what France actually is. Hmm. You're right. But I still have the option (　　　　)[8] having a native speaker as a roommate. In the dormitory? That might (　　　　)[9]. But I heard one student got a roommate who was (　　　　)[10] native French speaker, and they never talked. Oh, no. Yes, and another student got a non-native French-speaking roommate who (　　　　)[11] really friendly. Maybe it doesn't matter if my roommate is a native speaker or (　　　　)[12]. The same applies to a host family.

Hey, Kate! You dropped (　　　　)[13] receipt. Here. Thanks, Yasuko. It's so huge for a bag (　　　　)[14] chips. What a waste of paper! Yeah, but look at (　　　　)[15] the discount coupons. You can use them next (　　　　)[16] you're in the store, Kate. Seriously, Luke? Do you actually use those? It's so wasteful. (　　　　)[17], receipts might contain harmful chemicals, right Michael? Yeah, and that could mean they aren't recyclable. See? We should prohibit paper receipts. ( )[18] recently heard one city in the US might ban paper receipts by 2022. Really, Yasuko? But ( )[19] would that work? I need paper receipts as proof of purchase. Right. ( )[20] agree. What if I want to return something for ( )[21] refund? If this becomes law, Michael, shops will issue digital receipts via email instead of paper ( )[22]. Great. Really? Are you OK with giving your private email address to strangers? Well... yes. Anyway, paper receipts are safer, ( )[23] more people would rather have them. I don't know what ( )[24] think, Luke. You could request a paper receipt, I guess. No way! There should be NO paper option. Luke's right. I still prefer paper receipts.

問題英文の日本語訳を確認しよう。

ショウ，大丈夫？ どうしたの？ やあ，ジェーン。結局，フランス語を母国語とするホストファミリーが見つからないって分かったんだ。フランスへの留学プログラムのために。ホストファミリーを選んだんだね，寮ではなくて。まだだけどね。ネイティブのフランス語を話す家族を望んでいたんだけどね。どうして？ なんていうか，実際に話されるフランス語を経験したかったんだよね。ショウ，フランス語って，実は，いろいろあるんだよ。だろうね。でも，フランス語を母国語とするホストファミリーがいれば，本物の言語と本物のフランス文化を体験できると思ったんだよ。そもそも「本物」とは何だろう？ フランスは多様なのよ。多言語を話す家族と一緒にいれば，実際のフランスを実感できるかもしれないじゃない。うーん，そうだね。でも，まだ，もう1つのオプションがあるんだ。それは，ネイティブスピーカーをルームメイトとして迎えるっていうの。寮で？ それはうまくいくかもね。でも，こんなことを聞いたことがあるのよ。ある学生がいてね，その学生には，フランス語を母国語とするルームメイトがいたんだけど，一度も会話をしなかったって。あらまあ。そうなのよ。また，別の学生の話なんだけど，その学生には，フランス語が母国語ではないんだけど，とてもフレンドリーなルームメイトがいたのよ。ってことは，ルームメイトがネイティブスピーカーかどうかは関係ないのかもしれないね。ホストファミリーも同様だと思うよ。

やあ，ケイト！ レシート落としてるよ。これ。ヤスコ，ありがとう。ポテトチップスを一袋買っただけなのに，妙にそのレシート，大きいね。なんて紙の無駄なんでしょう。うん，でも割引クーポン，全部見てみてよ。次にその店に行ったときに使えるのよ，ケイト。ルーク，ほんとに？ 実際にそんなの使うの？ 無駄じゃない？ それに，レシートには有害な化学物質が含まれている可能性もあるんだよ。マイケル，そうでしょ？ そうだねえ，となると，リサイクルできないってことだね。でしょ？ だから紙のレシートを禁止すべきだよ。最近，聞いたんだけど，アメリカのある都市が2022年までに紙のレシートを禁止するかもしれないって。ヤスコ，本当？ でも，うまくいくのかな？ 私なら，ものを買った証明として紙のレシートがいると思うけどな。そうそう。同感。返品してお金を受け取りたい場合はどうすればいいのよ？ マイケル，これが法律になったら，店は電子メールでデジタルレシートを発行することになるよ。紙のレシートじゃなくって。いいじゃない。本当に？ 大丈夫なの？ 自分の個人メール住所をまったく知らない人に教えても？ まあ，そうだね。いずれにせよ，紙のレシートの方が安全だし，紙のレシートの方がいいって人の方が多いと思うよ。ルーク，どう考えていいか分からないよ。紙のレシートも要求できると思うんだけど。とんでもない！ 紙のオプションはないよ。ルークの方が正しいんじゃないかな。私はやっぱり紙のレシートの方が好き。

MET 2021 本（5）解答

解答付き英文を見ながら，英語の音声をもう一度聞いてみよう。

Are you all right, Sho? What's wrong? Hey, Jane. It turns out a native French-speaking (**host**)[1] family was not available... for my study abroad program in France. So (**you**)[2] chose a host family instead of the dormitory, huh? Not yet. (**I**)[3] was hoping for a native French-speaking family. Why? Well, I wanted to experience (**real**)[4] spoken French. Sho, there are many varieties of French. I guess. But with (**a**)[5] native French-speaking host family, I thought I could experience real language and real French culture. What's "real," anyway? France (**is**)[6] diverse. Staying with a multilingual family could give you a genuine feel (**of**)[7] what France actually is. Hmm. You're right. But I still have the option (**of**)[8] having a native speaker as a roommate. In the dormitory? That might (**work**)[9]. But I heard one student got a roommate who was (**a**)[10] native French speaker, and they never talked. Oh, no. Yes, and another student got a non-native French-speaking roommate who (**was**)[11] really friendly. Maybe it doesn't matter if my roommate is a native speaker or (**not**)[12]. The same applies to a host family.

Hey, Kate! You dropped (**your**)[13] receipt. Here. Thanks, Yasuko. It's so huge for a bag (**of**)[14] chips. What a waste of paper! Yeah, but look at (**all**)[15] the discount coupons. You can use them next (**time**)[16] you're in the store, Kate. Seriously, Luke? Do you actually use those? It's so wasteful. (**Also**)[17], receipts might contain harmful chemicals, right Michael? Yeah, and that could mean they aren't recyclable. See? We should prohibit paper receipts. (**I**)[18] recently heard one city in the US might ban paper receipts by 2022. Really, Yasuko? But (**how**)[19] would that work? I need paper receipts as proof of purchase. Right. (**I**)[20] agree. What if I want to return something for (**a**)[21] refund? If this becomes law, Michael, shops will issue digital receipts via email instead of paper (**ones**)[22]. Great. Really? Are you OK with giving your private email address to strangers? Well... yes. Anyway, paper receipts are safer, (**and**)[23] more people would rather have them. I don't know what (**to**)[24] think, Luke. You could request a paper receipt, I guess. No way! There should be NO paper option. Luke's right. I still prefer paper receipts.

MET 2022 本 (1)

英語の音声を聞きながら，（　　）の中に，英単語を入れてください。

There weren't very many people on the bus, (　　　　　)[1] I sat down. Susan, I left (　　　　　)[2] phone at home. Wait here. I'll be (　　　　　)[3]. I didn't lose my map of London. I've (　　　　　)[4] found it in my suitcase. Claire usually meets Thomas for lunch on Fridays, (　　　　　)[5] she's too busy this week. Kathy ate two pieces, (　　　　　)[6] Jon ate everything else. So, nothing's left. Look (　　　　　)[7] that bird on the lake. It's under (　　　　　)[8] tree. I prefer this one. There's no belt, (　　　　　)[9] it's longer. Oh, I forgot. Where should these towels go? In the basket on (　　　　　)[10] bottom shelf. The one beside the bottles? No, the other one. Where should the woman put (　　　　　)[11] towels? Are you ready to order, sir? Yes, I'd like the fried noodle (　　　　　)[12]. Certainly. Would you like rice with that? Well.... (　　　　　)[13] comes with two side dishes, so that's enough. What did (　　　　　)[14] man order? Can I put this shirt (　　　　　)[15] the dryer? No, look at the square symbol. It's crossed out. (　　　　　)[16] I have to iron it? Well, (　　　　　)[17] symbol shows that you can. Which picture shows what they (　　　　　)[18] looking at? I'd rather not sit near the (　　　　　)[19]. But not too near the screen, either. Isn't (　　　　　)[20] sound better at the back? Do you think (　　　　　)[21]? Let's sit there, then. Which seats will the speakers choose?

MET 2022（1）日本語訳

問題英文の日本語訳を確認しよう。

バスにはあまり人がいなかったので，座った。スーザン，携帯電話を家に忘れてきちゃった。ここで待ってて。戻ってくるから。ロンドンの地図，なくさなかったよ。たった今スーツケースの中に見つけたんだ。クレアは普通は金曜日にトーマスと会って，ランチをするが，今週はとても忙しい。キャシーは2きれ食べて，ジョンは残りをすべて食べた。だから，何も残ってない。あの鳥見て，湖に浮かんでる。木の下にいるよ。こっちのほうが好きだな。ベルトがなくて，長め。ああ，忘れてた。このタオルはどこに置けばいい？ 下の段のカゴの中。瓶の横の？ いや，もう1つの方。この女性はタオルをどこに置いたでしょうか？ ご注文はお決まりですか？ はい，焼きそばセットをお願いします。承知いたしました。それと一緒にご飯はいかがですか？ まあ，おかずが2品付いているので，これで十分です。その男性は何を注文しましたか？ このシャツを乾燥機に入れてもいい？ いえ，四角の記号を見て。バツ印が付いてる。このシャツ，アイロンをかけなきゃいけない？ この記号を見れば，大丈夫だって。どの写真が彼らが見ているものを示していますか？ 出口近くには座りたくない。でも，画面に近すぎるのもいや。後ろのほうが音が良くない？ そう思う？ じゃあ，そこに座ろう。この会話をしている人たちは，どの席を選ぶでしょうか？

MET 2022 本（1）解答

解答付き英文を見ながら，英語の音声をもう一度聞いてみよう。

There weren't very many people on the bus, (**so**)[1] I sat down. Susan, I left (**my**)[2] phone at home. Wait here. I'll be (**back**)[3]. I didn't lose my map of London. I've (**just**)[4] found it in my suitcase. Claire usually meets Thomas for lunch on Fridays, (**but**)[5] she's too busy this week. Kathy ate two pieces, (**and**)[6] Jon ate everything else. So, nothing's left. Look (**at**)[7] that bird on the lake. It's under (**the**)[8] tree. I prefer this one. There's no belt, (**and**)[9] it's longer. Oh, I forgot. Where should these towels go? In the basket on (**the**)[10] bottom shelf. The one beside the bottles? No, the other one. Where should the woman put (**the**)[11] towels? Are you ready to order, sir? Yes, I'd like the fried noodle (**set**)[12]. Certainly. Would you like rice with that? Well.... (**It**)[13] comes with two side dishes, so that's enough. What did (**the**)[14] man order? Can I put this shirt (**in**)[15] the dryer? No, look at the square symbol. It's crossed out. (**Do**)[16] I have to iron it? Well, (**this**)[17] symbol shows that you can. Which picture shows what they (**are**)[18] looking at? I'd rather not sit near the (**exit**)[19]. But not too near the screen, either. Isn't (**the**)[20] sound better at the back? Do you think (**so**)[21]? Let's sit there, then. Which seats will the speakers choose?

MET 2022 本 (2)

／ 28 点

英語の音声を聞きながら，（　　　）の中に，英単語を入れてください。

It's just about to rain. Then I'm leaving right now, (　　　)¹ I won't get wet. You can't get (　　　)² the train station before it starts raining. I think I can. Well, (　　　)³ rain won't last long anyway. I'm waiting here. Once (　　　)⁴ starts, I don't think it'll stop that soon. The doctor (　　　)⁵ I need to come back (　　　)⁶ two weeks. The first available appointment is March 2nd at 5. How's that? I'm afraid that's no (　　　)⁷. How about the next day? There are openings (　　　)⁸ 11:30 and 4. Which is better? Hmm, I guess I'll come in (　　　)⁹ morning. That's a nice handbag! Where did you get (　　　)¹⁰? At the new department store. I want (　　　)¹¹ buy one just like that for (　　　)¹² mother's birthday. Actually, I'm going there with my sister to-morrow to find a shoulder (　　　)¹³ for my aunt. Can I (　　　)¹⁴ with you? Of course. How do (　　　)¹⁵ get to the museum? You mean (　　　)¹⁶ new city museum? Yeah, the one featuring American art. That museum displays works (　　　)¹⁷ Asia, not from America. Really? I saw American art (　　　)¹⁸ their website once. That was a temporary exhibit, on (　　　)¹⁹ from another museum. Too bad. Hey, I can't log (　　　)²⁰. Did you put in the right password? Yes, (　　　)²¹ did. I retyped it several times. And is (　　　)²² username correct? I think so.... It's my student number, isn't it? Yes. But is (　　　)²³ your stu-dent number? Uh-oh, I entered two zeros instead of one. How was (　　　)²⁴ concert yesterday? Well, I enjoyed the performance a lot, but (　　　)²⁵ concert only lasted an hour. Oh, that's kind of short. (　　　)²⁶ much did you pay? About 10,000 yen. Wow, that's a (　　　)²⁷! Do you think it was worth that (　　　)²⁸? No, not really.

MET 2022（2）日本語訳

問題英文の日本語訳を確認しよう。

いまにも雨が降りそう。じゃあ，今から出発するから濡れないよ。駅に着くことはできないよ，雨が降り始める前には。できるって。まあ，いずれにしても雨は長くは降らないと思うから。ここで待ってるよ。一度降り始めたら，そうすぐには止まないと思うけどね。医者が言うんだよ。2 週間後にまた来いって。可能な予約ですが，3 月 2 日の 5 時です。どうですか？ ちょっと難しいです。次の日はどうでしょうか？ 11 時半と 4 時に空きがありますが，どちらがよろしいでしょうか？うーん，午前中には来られると思います。素敵なハンドバッグね！ どこで手に入れたの？ 新しいデパートで。母の誕生日に同じようなものを購入したいな。実は，明日，妹と一緒にそこに行くのよ。叔母のショルダーバッグを探しに。一緒にいってもいい？ もちろん。美術館へはどうやって行けばいいですか？ 新しい市立美術館のことですか？ そう，アメリカのアートを専門にしたのです。その美術館はアメリカじゃなくて，アジアの作品を展示しています。本当ですか？ 一度，アメリカのアートをウェブサイトで見たことがあります。それは別の美術館から借りた一時的な展示品でした。残念ですねえ。あらあ，ログインできない。正しいパスワードを入力した？ ええ。何べんも打ち直したし。ユーザー名は正しい？ そう思うんだけど。学生番号だよね？ ええ。でも，それはあなたの学生番号？ ああ，ゼロを 2 つ入力しちゃった。1 つじゃなくて。昨日のコンサートはどうだった？ そうねえ，とても楽しかったんだけど，コンサートはたったの 1 時間だったのよ。ああ，それはちょっと短いね。いくらかかったの？ 1 万円くらい。うわー，そりゃ大金だ！それだけの価値があったかな？ いや，そうとは言えないな。

MET 2022 本（2）解答

解答付き英文を見ながら，英語の音声をもう一度聞いてみよう。

It's just about to rain. Then I'm leaving right now, (**so**)[1] I won't get wet. You can't get (**to**)[2] the train station before it starts raining. I think I can. Well, (**the**)[3] rain won't last long anyway. I'm waiting here. Once (**it**)[4] starts, I don't think it'll stop that soon. The doctor (**says**)[5] I need to come back (**in**)[6] two weeks. The first available appointment is March 2nd at 5. How's that? I'm afraid that's no (**good**)[7]. How about the next day? There are openings (**at**)[8] 11:30 and 4. Which is better? Hmm, I guess I'll come in (**the**)[9] morning. That's a nice handbag! Where did you get (**it**)[10]? At the new department store. I want (**to**)[11] buy one just like that for (**my**)[12] mother's birthday. Actually, I'm going there with my sister tomorrow to find a shoulder (**bag**)[13] for my aunt. Can I (**go**)[14] with you? Of course. How do (**I**)[15] get to the museum? You mean (**the**)[16] new city museum? Yeah, the one featuring American art. That museum displays works (**from**)[17] Asia, not from America. Really? I saw American art (**on**)[18] their website once. That was a temporary exhibit, on (**loan**)[19] from another museum. Too bad. Hey, I can't log (**in**)[20]. Did you put in the right password? Yes, (**I**)[21] did. I retyped it several times. And is (**your**)[22] username correct? I think so.... It's my student number, isn't it? Yes. But is (**that**)[23] your student number? Uh-oh, I entered two zeros instead of one. How was (**the**)[24] concert yesterday? Well, I enjoyed the performance a lot, but (**the**)[25] concert only lasted an hour. Oh, that's kind of short. (**How**)[26] much did you pay? About 10,000 yen. Wow, that's a (**lot**)[27]! Do you think it was worth that (**much**)[28]? No, not really.

英語の音声を聞きながら，（　　）の中に，英単語を入れてください。

I always enjoy the holidays.　One of my happiest memories is about （　　　　）[1] snowy night just before Christmas.　As the hall clock struck nine, there was （　　　　）[2] loud knock at the door.　"Who could （　　　　）[3] be?" we wondered.　My father went to （　　　　）[4] door, and in a surprised voice we heard, "Oh, （　　　　）[5]... look who's here!"　We all ran to （　　　　）[6] hall, and there was my favorite uncle with （　　　　）[7] arms full of gifts.　He surprised us （　　　　）[8] a visit.　Then, he helped us decorate our Christmas （　　　　）[9].　We had so much fun.　（　　　　）[10] are all the items that were donated （　　　　）[11] week.　Please help me sort them （　　　　）[12] the proper boxes.　First, summer clothes go into Box 1, whether they （　　　　）[13] for men or for women.　In （　　　　）[14] same way, all winter clothes for men （　　　　）[15] women go into Box 2.　Box 3 is （　　　　）[16] children's clothes, regardless of the season they're worn in. Shoes and （　　　　）[17] should be put into Box 4.　All other items （　　　　）[18] into Box 5.

There are so many books （　　　　）[19] choose from, but one I think would be good （　　　　）[20] a science fiction novel, *Exploring Space and Beyond*, that was published last month.　It （　　　　）[21] be read in one sitting because it's just 150 pages long.　（　　　　）[22] read a review online about a book that （　　　　）[23] published earlier this year, titled *Farming as a Family*.　It's a true story about a （　　　　）[24] who decided to move with his family （　　　　）[25] the countryside to farm.　It's an easy （　　　　）[26]... around

200 pages. I know a really good autobiography called *My Life as a Pop Star*. It's 300 pages in length. (   )^{27} think it would be an interesting discussion topic for our group. (   )^{28} learned a lot when I read (   )^{29} several years ago. I heard about a new book, *Winning at the Olympics*. (   )^{30} features Olympic athletes who won medals. It has so (   )^{31} interesting photographs and some really amazing true-life stories. It's 275 pages long.

MET 2022（3）日本語訳

問題英文の日本語訳を確認しよう。

私はいつも休日を楽しんでいます。私の最も幸せな思い出の1つは，クリスマス直前の雪の夜のことです。ホールの時計が9時を打った時，ドアをノックする大きな音が聞こえました。「誰だろう？」と思いました。父はドアのところに行きました。父が驚いた声でこう言うのが聞こえました。「おやおや，誰が来たかと思ったら！」私たちは皆ホールに走って行きました。私の大好きな叔父が両手にプレゼントをいっぱい抱えて立っていました。叔父はこっそり訪れて，私達を驚かせようとしたのです。それから，クリスマスツリーの飾り付けを手伝ってくれました。とても楽しかった思い出です。品物はすべてこちらです。先週ご寄付いただいた品物。適切な箱に仕分けるのを手伝ってください。まず，夏服はボックス1に入れてください。男性用，女性用を問わず。同様に，すべての冬服は，男性用，女性用を問わず，ボックス2に入れてください。ボックス3は子供服です。季節に関係なく。靴とバッグはボックス4に。その他の品物はすべてボックス5に。

選べる本はたくさんありますが，私が良いと思うのは，『Exploring Space and Beyond』です。先月出版されたSF小説の。一気に読めます。150ページしかないので。私は，書評をオンラインで読みました。今年初めに出版された本で，『Farming as a Family』というタイトルの本です。これは，ある男性の実話です。家族とともに田舎に移住して農業をすることを決意した男性の。読みやすい本です。200ページくらい。私は，とても良い自伝を知っています。『My Life as a Pop Star』という本です。300ページあります。それは，おもしろい議論のテーマになると思います。私たちのグループにとって。とても勉強になりました。数年前に読んで。新しい本『Winning at the Olympics』について聞きました。オリンピック選手が登場します。メダルを獲得した。興味深い写真がたくさんあり，本当に驚くべき実話がいくつかあります。275ページあります。

MET 2022 本 (3) 解答

解答付き英文を見ながら，英語の音声をもう一度聞いてみよう。

I always enjoy the holidays. One of my happiest memories is about (**a**)[1] snowy night just before Christmas. As the hall clock struck nine, there was (**a**)[2] loud knock at the door. "Who could (**it**)[3] be?" we wondered. My father went to (**the**)[4] door, and in a surprised voice we heard, "Oh, (**my**)[5]... look who's here!" We all ran to (**the**)[6] hall, and there was my favorite uncle with (**his**)[7] arms full of gifts. He surprised us (**with**)[8] a visit. Then, he helped us decorate our Christmas (**tree**)[9]. We had so much fun. (**Here**)[10] are all the items that were donated (**last**)[11] week. Please help me sort them (**into**)[12] the proper boxes. First, summer clothes go into Box 1, whether they (**are**)[13] for men or for women. In (**the**)[14] same way, all winter clothes for men (**and**)[15] women go into Box 2. Box 3 is (**for**)[16] children's clothes, regardless of the season they're worn in. Shoes and (**bags**)[17] should be put into Box 4. All other items (**go**)[18] into Box 5.

There are so many books (**to**)[19] choose from, but one I think would be good (**is**)[20] a science fiction novel, *Exploring Space and Beyond*, that was published last month. It (**can**)[21] be read in one sitting because it's just 150 pages long. (**I**)[22] read a review online about a book that (**was**)[23] published earlier this year, titled *Farming as a Family*. It's a true story about a (**man**)[24] who decided to move with his family (**to**)[25] the countryside to farm. It's an easy (**read**)[26]... around 200 pages. I know a really good autobiography called *My Life as a Pop Star*. It's 300 pages in length. (**I**)[27] think it would be an interesting discussion topic for our group. (**I**)[28] learned a lot when I read (**it**)[29] several years ago. I heard about a new book, *Winning at the Olympics*. (**It**)[30] features Olympic athletes who won medals. It has so (**many**)[31] interesting photographs and some really amazing true-life stories. It's 275 pages long.

MET 2022 本 (4)

英語の音声を聞きながら，（　）の中に，英単語を入れてください。

Today I'll introduce a recent work model based on "gig work." Do you
(　　　　)[1] this term? This model utilizes the spread of smartphones
(　　　　)[2] the internet. It enables businesses to connect with and
(　　　　)[3] freelance workers through digital platforms. These workers are
called gig workers, who do individual jobs, (　　　　)[4] gigs, on short-term
contracts. Let's look at some benefits (　　　　)[5] the gig work model.
This model is attractive (　　　　)[6] companies because they can save on
operating costs, and (　　　　)[7] can easily hire a more skilled workforce
through digital platforms. The workers (　　　　)[8] the opportunity to control the numbers and types of projects according (　　　　)[9] their preferences, with the freedom to choose their schedule and workload. However,
their income can (　　　　)[10] unstable because it is based on individual
payments instead of a regular salary. (　　　　)[11] gig work model is expanding to include various types of (　　　　)[12]. It has become common
for local service jobs such (　　　　)[13] taxi and delivery drivers. There is
now increasing demand for highly specialized project (　　　　)[14], not only
domestically but also internationally. For example, (　　　　)[15] company
that needs help with its advertising can (　　　　)[16] international consultants who work remotely in different countries. In fact, (　　　　)[17] large
number of U.S. companies are already taking advantage of digital platforms
to employ an international workforce. (　　　　)[18] gig work model is challenging us to rethink (　　　　)[19] concepts of permanent employment, and
full-time and part-time work. Working on (　　　　)[20] contract basis for

multiple companies may give gig workers additional income while maintaining their work-life balance. As ( )^{21} and more people enter the gig job market, ( )^{22} work model will undoubtedly expand as a work model ( )^{23} future generations. The growing effects of gig work on employment ( )^{24} markets differ regionally. Look at the two graphs containing data from ( )^{25} major English-language online labor platforms. They show the top five countries in terms ( )^{26} percentages of all gig employers and gig employees. ( )^{27} trend can we see here?

MET 2022（4）日本語訳

問題英文の日本語訳を確認しよう。

今回は，最近の働き方モデルをご紹介します。「ギグワーク」をベースにしたモデルです。この「ギグワーク」という用語を知っていますか？ このモデルは，スマートフォンとインターネットの普及を活用したモデルです。これにより，企業は，フリーランス労働者とつながり，雇用できるようになります。デジタルプラットフォームを通じて。これらの労働者はギグワーカーと呼ばれ，個人の仕事，つまりギグを行います。短期契約で。ギグワークモデルの利点をいくつか見てみましょう。このモデルは，企業にとって魅力的です。というのも，運営コストが節約でき，デジタルプラットフォームを通じてより熟練した労働力を簡単に雇用できるからです。また，従業員も，さまざまなオプションを選ぶ機会があります。例えば，好みに応じてプロジェクトの数や種類を選ぶことができます。その際，自分のスケジュールと作業量を自由に選択できます。しかしながら，収入が不安定になる可能性もあります。というのも，収入は，個人の支払いに基づいているからです。定期的な給与ではなくて。ギグワークモデルはさまざまな職種に広がりつつあります。地域のサービス業では一般的になってきています。例えば，タクシーや配送ドライバーなどです。現在，高度に専門性の高いプロジェクト業務への需要が高まっています。国内のみならず海外においても。例えば，広告に関するサポートが必要な企業は，国際的なコンサルタントを雇うことができます。さまざまな国でリモートで働くコンサルタントです。実際，多くの米国企業がすでに国際的な労働力を雇用しています。デジタルプラットフォームを活用して。ギグワークモデルは，私たちに次の概念を再考するよう求めています。「終身雇用」と「フルタイム労働とパートタイム労働」。複数の企業と契約ベースで働くことで，ギグワーカーは，追加収入を得る可能性があります。ワークライフバランスを維持しながら。ギグジョブ市場に参入する人が増えるにつれ，このワークモデルは間違いなく将来世代のワークモデルとして拡大していくでしょう。ギグワークが雇用と市場に与える影響の拡大は地域によって異なります。2つのグラフを見てください。主要な英語のオンライン労働プラットフォームからのデータを含むグラフです。これらは，上位5か国を示しています。すべてのギグ雇用主とギグ従業員の割合に関する上位5か国です。これらのグラフにおいて，どのような傾向が見られるでしょうか？

MET 2022 本（4）解答

解答付き英文を見ながら，英語の音声をもう一度聞いてみよう。

Today I'll introduce a recent work model based on "gig work." Do you (**know**)[1] this term? This model utilizes the spread of smartphones (**and**)[2] the internet. It enables businesses to connect with and (**hire**)[3] freelance workers through digital platforms. These workers are called gig workers, who do individual jobs, (**or**)[4] gigs, on short-term contracts. Let's look at some benefits (**of**)[5] the gig work model. This model is attractive (**to**)[6] companies because they can save on operating costs, and (**they**)[7] can easily hire a more skilled workforce through digital platforms. The workers (**have**)[8] the opportunity to control the numbers and types of projects according (**to**)[9] their preferences, with the freedom to choose their schedule and workload. However, their income can (**be**)[10] unstable because it is based on individual payments instead of a regular salary. (**The**)[11] gig work model is expanding to include various types of (**work**)[12]. It has become common for local service jobs such (**as**)[13] taxi and delivery drivers. There is now increasing demand for highly specialized project (**work**)[14], not only domestically but also internationally. For example, (**a**)[15] company that needs help with its advertising can (**hire**)[16] international consultants who work remotely in different countries. In fact, (**a**)[17] large number of U.S. companies are already taking advantage of digital platforms to employ an international workforce. (**The**)[18] gig work model is challenging us to rethink (**the**)[19] concepts of permanent employment, and full-time and part-time work. Working on (**a**)[20] contract basis for multiple companies may give gig workers additional income while maintaining their work-life balance. As (**more**)[21] and more people enter the gig job market, (**this**)[22] work model will undoubtedly expand as a work model (**for**)[23] future generations. The growing effects of gig work on employment (**and**)[24] markets differ regionally. Look at the two graphs containing data from (**the**)[25] major English-language online labor platforms. They show the top five countries in terms (**of**)[26] percentages of all gig employers and gig employees. (**What**)[27] trend can we see here?

MET 2022 本 (5)

英語の音声を聞きながら，（　）の中に，英単語を入れてください。

Oh, no. I'm out of butter. What are you making, Julia? (　　　　)^1 was going to make an omelet. How about using olive (　　　　)^2 instead? But, Tom, the recipe says to use butter. (　　　　)^3 don't you just change the recipe? I don't like cooking (　　　　)^4 way. I just throw together whatever is in (　　　　)^5 refrigerator. For me, cooking is a creative act. (　　　　)^6 for me. I need to follow (　　　　)^7 recipe. I like to think about how the ingredients (　　　　)^8 combine. I don't have to think about it if (　　　　)^9 follow a recipe precisely. I use measuring spoons, a measuring cup, (　　　　)^{10} a step-by-step recipe. You like my food, don't (　　　　)^{11}? Absolutely. Your beef stew is especially delicious. See? There (　　　　)^{12} something to be said for sticking to (　　　　)^{13} plan. And without butter I cannot make an omelet. OK. (　　　　)^{14}, what are you going to do (　　　　)^{15} those eggs? How about boiled eggs? Where's the recipe?

Hey, Brian. Look (　　　　)^{16} that beautiful red coral necklace. Ooh... expensive. Anne, red coral is endangered. They shouldn't (　　　　)^{17} selling that. So, how are they going (　　　　)^{18} make money? There're lots of ways to (　　　　)^{19} that if we consider ecotourism. Yeah... ecotourism.... What do (　　　　)^{20} think, Donna? Well, Anne, ecotourism supports the local economy in a good way while protecting (　　　　)^{21} environment. Right. So, we shouldn't buy coral; it'll become extinct. Oh, come on, Brian. (　　　　)^{22} about the people relying on the coral reefs?

But, Anne, those coral reefs take millions (　　　　　)^{23} years to regrow. We should support more sustainable ways to (　　　　　)^{24} money. Hey Hiro, didn't you buy some photos of coral reefs? Yeah, taken by (　　　　　)^{25} local photographer. They are beautiful. That's ecotourism. We shouldn't impact the environment so (　　　　　)^{26}. But that's not enough to support people relying on coral reefs for income. Hiro (　　　　　)^{27} a point. They should find other ways to (　　　　　)^{28} money while still preserving the reefs. I'm not sure if we (　　　　　)^{29} in a position to tell them (　　　　　)^{30} they should make their money. Anne's right. Selling coral is their local tradition. We should respect that. (　　　　　)^{31}, at the expense of the environment, Hiro? The environment (　　　　　)^{32} important, but if we protect it, I don't think (　　　　　)^{33} economy is supported. Anyway, we're on vacation. It's a nice day. Let's (　　　　　)^{34} the beach!

MET 2022 (5) 日本語訳

問題英文の日本語訳を確認しよう。

あれまあ。バターがなくなっちゃった。ジュリア，何作ってるの？ オムレツを作るつもりだったんだけど。代わりにオリーブオイルを使ってみたら？ でもトム，レシピーにはバターを使えって書いてあるよ。ちょっとレシピーを変えてみたら？ そんな具合に料理をするのが好きじゃないんだけど。私なら，冷蔵庫にあるものを混ぜるだけ。私にとっては，料理はいつも新しいものを作るもの。私は違うんだなあ。レシピーに従うタイプなんだ。私は，材料をどう組み合わせるか考えるのが好き。レシピー通りに作れば何も考えなくて済むじゃない。私は，計量スプーン，計量カップ，そして段取り通りのレシピーを使うタイプ。私が作る食べ物，好きだよね？ そりゃあもう，絶対的に。ビーフシチューはとりわけ。でしょ？ 計画通りことを進めることは，意味があるの。そしてバターがなければオムレツは作れない。わかったわ。じゃあ，その卵はどうするつもり？ ゆで卵はどうかな？ レシピーはどこだっけ？

やあ，ブライアン。見てよ。この美しい赤珊瑚のネックレス。ああ…値がすごい。アン，赤サンゴは絶滅の危機に瀕してるのよ。販売すべきじゃないと思うんだけど。じゃあ，どうやってお金を稼ぐの？ 方法はたくさんあるよ。エコツーリズムを考えればね。まあ，エコツーリズムね。ドナ，どう思う？ そうねえ，アン，エコツーリズムは，地元経済を良い形でサポートするよね。環境を保護しながら。そうそう。だから，私たちはサンゴを買うべきじゃない。絶滅しちゃうんだから。おいおい，ブライアン。サンゴ礁に依存している人は，どうしたらいいのよ？ でも，アン，そのサンゴ礁は再生するのに何百万年もかかるんだよ。持続可能な方法をサポートする必要があるんじゃないのかなあ，お金を稼ぐための。ねえ，ヒロ，サンゴ礁の写真を買わなかった？ ええ，地元の写真家が撮ったものよ。素晴らしい写真よ。それがエコツーリズムなの。私たちは環境に影響を与えるべきじゃない。でも，それだけではサンゴ礁に収入を依存している人を支えるには，十分じゃない。ヒロの言うことも一理あるよ。彼らはサンゴ礁を保護しながらお金を稼ぐ他の方法を見つける必要があるよね。私たちが彼らにどうやってお金を稼ぐべきか教える立場にあるかどうかは分からないなあ。アンの言うとおり。サンゴを売るのは彼らの地元の伝統。それを尊重すべきよ。でも，ヒロ，環境を犠牲にしてまで？環境は大切だけど，それを守っているだけでは経済は支えられないんじゃないかな。とにかく，私たちは休暇中。今日もいい日。海に行こう！

MET 2022 本 (5) 解答

解答付き英文を見ながら，英語の音声をもう一度聞いてみよう。

Oh, no. I'm out of butter. What are you making, Julia? (**I**)[1] was going to make an omelet. How about using olive (**oil**)[2] instead? But, Tom, the recipe says to use butter. (**Why**)[3] don't you just change the recipe? I don't like cooking (**that**)[4] way. I just throw together whatever is in (**the**)[5] refrigerator. For me, cooking is a creative act. (**Not**)[6] for me. I need to follow (**a**)[7] recipe. I like to think about how the ingredients (**will**)[8] combine. I don't have to think about it if (**I**)[9] follow a recipe precisely. I use measuring spoons, a measuring cup, (**and**)[10] a step-by-step recipe. You like my food, don't (**you**)[11]? Absolutely. Your beef stew is especially delicious. See? There (**is**)[12] something to be said for sticking to (**a**)[13] plan. And without butter I cannot make an omelet. OK. (**So**)[14], what are you going to do (**with**)[15] those eggs? How about boiled eggs? Where's the recipe?

Hey, Brian. Look (**at**)[16] that beautiful red coral necklace. Ooh... expensive. Anne, red coral is endangered. They shouldn't (**be**)[17] selling that. So, how are they going (**to**)[18] make money? There're lots of ways to (**do**)[19] that if we consider ecotourism. Yeah... ecotourism.... What do (**you**)[20] think, Donna? Well, Anne, ecotourism supports the local economy in a good way while protecting (**the**)[21] environment. Right. So, we shouldn't buy coral; it'll become extinct. Oh, come on, Brian. (**How**)[22] about the people relying on the coral reefs? But, Anne, those coral reefs take millions (**of**)[23] years to regrow. We should support more sustainable ways to (**make**)[24] money. Hey Hiro, didn't you buy some photos of coral reefs? Yeah, taken by (**a**)[25] local photographer. They are beautiful. That's ecotourism. We shouldn't impact the environment so (**much**)[26]. But that's not enough to support people relying on coral reefs for income. Hiro (**has**)[27] a point. They should find other ways to (**make**)[28] money while still preserving the reefs. I'm not sure if we (**are**)[29] in a position to tell them (**how**)[30] they should make their money. Anne's right. Selling coral is their local tradition. We should respect that. (**But**)[31], at the expense of the environment, Hiro? The environment (**is**)[32] important, but if we protect it, I don't think (**the**)[33] economy is supported. Anyway, we're on vacation. It's a nice day. Let's (**hit**)[34] the beach!

MET 2023 本 (1)

英語の音声を聞きながら，（　　）の中に，英単語を入れてください。

Sam, the TV is too loud. I'm working. (　　　　　)[1] you close the door? I've already washed the (　　　　　)[2], but I haven't started cleaning the pan. (　　　　)[3] at this postcard my uncle sent (　　　　　)[4] from Canada. There are twenty students in the classroom, (　　　　)[5] two more will come after lunch. There's not (　　　　)[6] tea left in the bottle. (　　　　)[7] can't see any cows. Oh, I (　　　　)[8] one behind the fence. I'm over here. I'm wearing black pants and holding (　　　　)[9] skateboard. This avatar with the glasses must (　　　　)[10] you! Why, because I'm holding my favorite drink? Of course! (　　　　)[11] you always have your computer with (　　　　)[12]. You're right! Which avatar is the woman's? Plastic bottles go in (　　　　)[13], and paper cups here. How about (　　　　)[14], then? Should I put this (　　　　)[15] here? No, that one is for glass. (　　　　)[16] it over here. OK. Which item (　　　　)[17] the woman holding? How about this pair? No, tying shoelaces takes (　　　　)[18] much time. Well, this other style is popular. These (　　　　)[19] 50% off, too. Nice! I'll take (　　　　)[20]. Which pair of shoes will the (　　　　)[21] buy? Where shall we meet? Well, I (　　　　)[22] to get some food before (　　　　)[23] game. And I need (　　　　)[24] use a locker. Then, let's meet there. Where (　　　　)[25] they meet up before the (　　　　)[26]?

MET 2023（1）日本語訳

問題英文の日本語訳を確認しよう。

サム，テレビの音が大きすぎ。ちょっと仕事してんのよ。ドアを閉めてくれる？　もうボウルは洗い終わったけど，まだフライパンは洗い始めてないよ。このポストカードを見てください。叔父がカナダから私に送ってくれたもの。教室には生徒が 20 人いるけど，昼食後にさらに 2 人来るよ。ボトルにお茶がほとんど残ってない。牛の姿は見えない。ああ，柵の後ろに一匹いる。ここにいるよ。黒いズボンを履いてスケートボードを持ってるよ。このメガネをかけたアバターはきっと君だね！　なんで？　私が好きな飲み物を持ってるから？　もちろん！　そして，いつもコンピューターを持ち歩いてる。正解！　その女性のアバターはどれですか？　ペットボトルはここに，紙コップはここに入れます。じゃあ，これは？　これをここに入れていいかな？　いや，それはガラス用。ここに置いてください。了解。その女性が持っているものはどれですか？　この靴はどうかな？　いや，靴紐を結ぶのに時間がかかりすぎる。まあ，この別のスタイルが人気ね。これも 50% オフ。素晴らしい！　それいただきます。その男性はどの靴を買うでしょうか？　どこで会おう？　えーっと，試合前に何か食べたいな。私は，ロッカーを使わなきゃならない。じゃあ，そこで会おう。彼らは試合前にどこに集合しますか？

MET 2023 本（1）解答

解答付き英文を見ながら，英語の音声をもう一度聞いてみよう。

Sam, the TV is too loud. I'm working. (**Can**)[1] you close the door? I've already washed the (**bowl**)[2], but I haven't started cleaning the pan. (**Look**)[3] at this postcard my uncle sent (**me**)[4] from Canada. There are twenty students in the classroom, (**and**)[5] two more will come after lunch. There's not (**much**)[6] tea left in the bottle. (**I**)[7] can't see any cows. Oh, I (**see**)[8] one behind the fence. I'm over here. I'm wearing black pants and holding (**a**)[9] skateboard. This avatar with the glasses must (**be**)[10] you! Why, because I'm holding my favorite drink? Of course! (**And**)[11] you always have your computer with (**you**)[12]. You're right! Which avatar is the woman's? Plastic bottles go in (**here**)[13], and paper cups here. How about (**this**)[14], then? Should I put this (**in**)[15] here? No, that one is for glass. (**Put**)[16] it over here. OK. Which item (**is**)[17] the woman holding? How about this pair? No, tying shoelaces takes (**too**)[18] much time. Well, this other style is popular. These (**are**)[19] 50% off, too. Nice! I'll take (**them**)[20]. Which pair of shoes will the (**man**)[21] buy? Where shall we meet? Well, I (**want**)[22] to get some food before (**the**)[23] game. And I need (**to**)[24] use a locker. Then, let's meet there. Where (**will**)[25] they meet up before the (**game**)[26]?

MET 2023 本（2）

英語の音声を聞きながら，（　　）の中に，英単語を入れてください。

Excuse me. I'd like to go (　　　　　)[1] Central Station. What's the best way to (　　　　)[2] there? After you take the Green Line, (　　　　)[3] transfer to the Blue Line (　　　　)[4] the Yellow Line at Riverside Station. Can (　　　　)[5] also take the Red (　　　　)[6] first? Usually that's faster, but it's closed for maintenance. Would you like (　　　　)[7] go out for dinner? Well, I'm not (　　　　)[8]. What about an Indian restaurant? You know, (　　　　)[9] like Indian food, but we shouldn't spend (　　　　)[10] much money this week. Then, (　　　　)[11] don't we just cook it ourselves, instead? That's (　　　　)[12] better idea! I can't find my dictionary! (　　　　)[13] did you use it (　　　　)[14]? In class? No, but I took (　　　　)[15] out of my backpack this morning (　　　　)[16] the bus to check my homework. (　　　　)[17] must have left it there. (　　　　)[18] driver will take it to (　　　　)[19] office. Oh, I'll call the office, then. How (　　　　)[20] your first week of classes? Good! I'm enjoying university (　　　　)[21]. So, are you originally from (　　　　)[22]? I mean, London? Yes, but my family moved (　　　　)[23] Germany after I was born. Then, (　　　　)[24] must be fluent in German. Yes. That's right. How (　　　　)[25] you? Well, I have a runny (　　　　)[26]. I always suffer from allergies in the spring. (　　　　)[27] you have some medicine? No, but I'll (　　　　)[28] by the drugstore on my (　　　　)[29] home to get my regular allergy pills. (　　　　)[30] should leave the office early. Yes, I think I'll leave now. What (　　　　)[31] cute dog! Thanks. Do you (　　　　)[32] a pet? I'm planning to get (　　　　)[33] cat. Do you want (　　　　)[34] adopt or buy one? What do (　　　　)[35] mean by 'adopt'? Instead of buying one at (　　　　)[36] petshop, you could give a new (　　　　)[37] to a rescued pet. That's a (　　　　)[38] idea. I'll do that!

MET 2023（2）日本語訳

問題英文の日本語訳を確認しよう。

すみません。中央駅に行きたいのですが。そこに行くのに一番いい方法は何ですか？ グリーンラインに乗ったら，リバーサイド駅でブルーラインまたはイエローラインに乗り換えてください。先にレッドラインに乗ってもいいですか？ 普通は，その方が早いんですが，修理のために閉鎖されています。夕食に出かけない？ えーっと，どうしよう。インド料理はどう？ あのー，インド料理は好きなんだけど，今週はお金を使いすぎないようにしてるんだ。それなら，自分たちで作らない？ そりゃいい！ 辞書が見つからないよお！ 最後にいつ使ったの？ クラスで？ いや，でも今朝，バスの中でリュックから取り出したんだよな。宿題を確認するために。じゃあ，バスに置いてきたに違いないよ。運転手が事務所まで届けますよ。ああ，じゃあ，事務所に電話してみるね。最初の一週間の授業はどうだった？ よかったよ！ ここでの大学生活，楽しんでます。じゃあ，もともとここの出身なの？ つまり，ロンドン？ ええ，家族はドイツに移住したんですよ，私が生まれてから。じゃあ，ドイツ語が流暢なんだね。ええ。まあまあ。元気？ なんていうか，鼻水が出るんだよね。春になるといつもアレルギーに悩まされるんだ。何か薬はあるかな？ いや，でも，帰りに薬局に寄るよ。いつものアレルギーの薬を買うために。じゃあ，早くオフィスを出たほうがいいね。うん，もう出るよ。なんて可愛い犬！ ありがとう。ペットを飼ってる？ 猫を飼う予定。里親になりたい，それとも買いたい？「里親になる」って，どういう意味？ ペットショップで購入する代わりに，保護されたペットを新しい家に迎えるってこと。それは良い考えだ。そうしよう！

MET 2023 本（2）解答

解答付き英文を見ながら，英語の音声をもう一度聞いてみよう。

Excuse me. I'd like to go (**to**)[1] Central Station. What's the best way to (**get**)[2] there? After you take the Green Line, (**just**)[3] transfer to the Blue Line (**or**)[4] the Yellow Line at Riverside Station. Can (**I**)[5] also take the Red (**Line**)[6] first? Usually that's faster, but it's closed for maintenance. Would you like (**to**)[7] go out for dinner? Well, I'm not (**sure**)[8]. What about an Indian restaurant? You know, (**I**)[9] like Indian food, but we shouldn't spend (**too**)[10] much money this week. Then, (**why**)[11] don't we just cook it ourselves, instead? That's (**a**)[12] better idea! I can't find my dictionary! (**When**)[13] did you use it (**last**)[14]? In class? No, but I took (**it**)[15] out of my backpack this morning (**in**)[16] the bus to check my homework. (**You**)[17] must have left it there. (**The**)[18] driver will take it to (**the**)[19] office. Oh, I'll call the office, then. How (**was**)[20] your first week of classes? Good! I'm enjoying university (**here**)[21]. So, are you originally from (**here**)[22]? I mean, London? Yes, but my family moved (**to**)[23] Germany after I was born. Then, (**you**)[24] must be fluent in German. Yes. That's right. How (**are**)[25] you? Well, I have a runny (**nose**)[26]. I always suffer from allergies in the spring. (**Do**)[27] you have some medicine? No, but I'll (**drop**)[28] by the drugstore on my (**way**)[29] home to get my regular allergy pills. (**You**)[30] should leave the office early. Yes, I think I'll leave now. What (**a**)[31] cute dog! Thanks. Do you (**have**)[32] a pet? I'm planning to get (**a**)[33] cat. Do you want (**to**)[34] adopt or buy one? What do (**you**)[35] mean by 'adopt'? Instead of buying one at (**a**)[36] petshop, you could give a new (**home**)[37] to a rescued pet. That's a (**good**)[38] idea. I'll do that!

MET 2023 本 (3)

英語の音声を聞きながら，（　　）の中に，英単語を入れてください。

Each year we survey our graduating students (　　　　)[1] why they chose their future jobs. We compared (　　　　)[2] results for 2011 and 2021. The four most popular factors (　　　　)[3] "content of work," "income," "location," and "working hours." The graph shows that "content (　　　)[4] work" increased the most. "Income" decreased a little (　　　)[5] 2021 compared with 2011. Although "location" was the second most chosen answer (　　　)[6] 2011, it dropped significantly in 2021. Finally, "working hours" was chosen slightly more (　　　)[7] graduates in 2021. We are delighted to announce (　　　)[8] prizes! Please look at the summary of (　　　)[9] results on your screen. First, the top (　　　)[10] in Stage A will be awarded medals. The (　　　)[11] team in Stage B will also receive medals. (　　　)[12], the team that got (　　　)[13] highest final rank will win the champion's trophies. (　　　)[14] members not winning any medals or trophies will receive (　　　)[15] game from our online store. The prizes (　　　)[16] be sent to everyone next (　　　)[17].

Hi there! Charlie, here. I'll work to increase the opening hours (　　　)[18] the computer room. Also, there should be (　　　)[19] events for all students. Finally, our student athletes need energy! (　　　)[20] I'll push for more meat options (　　　)[21] the cafeteria. Hello! I'm Jun. I think school meals would be healthier if (　　　)[22] cafeteria increased vegetarian choices. The computer lab should also be (　　　)[23] longer, especially in the afternoons. Finally, our school should have fewer events.

(   )^{24} should concentrate on homework and club activities! Hi guys! I'm Nancy. I support (   )^{25} school giving all students computers; then we wouldn't need (   )^{26} lab! I also think the cafeteria should bring (   )^{27} our favorite fried chicken. And school events need expanding. It's important for (   )^{28} students to get together! Hey everybody! I'm Philip. First, I don't think there are enough events (   )^{29} students. We should do more together! Next, (   )^{30} should be able to use (   )^{31} computer lab at the weekends, too. (   )^{32}, vegans like me need more vegetable-only meals (   )^{33} our cafeteria.

MET 2023 (3) 日本語訳

問題英文の日本語訳を確認しよう。

毎年，卒業していく学生にアンケートを実施する。将来の仕事を選んだ理由について。2011 年と 2021 年の結果を比較した。多かった項目は次の 4 つ。「仕事内容」「収入」「勤務地」「労働時間」の 4 つだった。グラフを見ると，「仕事内容」が最も増えていることが分かる。2021 年は 2011 年に比べて「収入」が若干減少した。2011 年には「勤務地」が 2 番目に多く選ばれた回答だったが，2021 年には大きく減少した。最後に，「労働時間」は，2021 年の卒業生の回答が若干増えた。賞品を発表します！ 画面上の結果の概要を確認してください。まず，ステージ A の優勝チームにメダルが与えられます。ステージ B の優勝チームにもメダルが与えられます。次に，最終順位が最も高かったチームがチャンピオンのトロフィーを獲得します。メダルやトロフィーを 1 つも獲得していないチームメンバーには，オンラインストアからゲームが提供されます。賞品は来週全員に発送されます。

こんにちは！ チャーリーです。コンピューター室の開館時間を増やすよう努めます。また，全学生向けのイベントをもっと増やすべきです。最後に，学生アスリートにはエネルギーが必要です。だから私はカフェテリアでもっと肉が食べられるよう働きかけます。こんにちは！ ジュンです。学校給食は，もっと健康的になるんじゃないかと思います。食堂でベジタリアンの選択肢が増えたら。コンピューター室も，もっと長く開いている必要があります。特に午後は。最後に，私たちの学校ではイベントを減らす必要があります。宿題と部活動に集中しましょう！ こんにちは，みんな！ ナンシーです。私は学校が全生徒にコンピューターを与えることを支持します。そうすればコンピューター室は必要なくなるでしょう！ また，食堂は，私たちの大好きなフライドチキンを復活させるべきだと思います。そして学校行事も拡大する必要があります。生徒全員が一致団結することが大切です！ やあ，みんな！ フィリップです。まず，学生向けのイベントが十分ではないと思います。もっとイベントを一緒にやるべきです！ 次は，週末にもコンピューター室を使えるようにする必要があります。また，私のようなビーガンには，カフェテリアで野菜のみの食事がもっと必要です。

MET 2023 本（3）解答

解答付き英文を見ながら，英語の音声をもう一度聞いてみよう。

Each year we survey our graduating students (**on**)[1] why they chose their future jobs. We compared (**the**)[2] results for 2011 and 2021. The four most popular factors (**were**)[3] "content of work," "income," "location," and "working hours." The graph shows that "content (**of**)[4] work" increased the most. "Income" decreased a little (**in**)[5] 2021 compared with 2011. Although "location" was the second most chosen answer (**in**)[6] 2011, it dropped significantly in 2021. Finally, "working hours" was chosen slightly more (**by**)[7] graduates in 2021. We are delighted to announce (**the**)[8] prizes! Please look at the summary of (**the**)[9] results on your screen. First, the top (**team**)[10] in Stage A will be awarded medals. The (**top**)[11] team in Stage B will also receive medals. (**Next**)[12], the team that got (**the**)[13] highest final rank will win the champion's trophies. (**Team**)[14] members not winning any medals or trophies will receive (**a**)[15] game from our online store. The prizes (**will**)[16] be sent to everyone next (**week**)[17].

Hi there! Charlie, here. I'll work to increase the opening hours (**of**)[18] the computer room. Also, there should be (**more**)[19] events for all students. Finally, our student athletes need energy! (**So**)[20] I'll push for more meat options (**in**)[21] the cafeteria. Hello! I'm Jun. I think school meals would be healthier if (**our**)[22] cafeteria increased vegetarian choices. The computer lab should also be (**open**)[23] longer, especially in the afternoons. Finally, our school should have fewer events. (**We**)[24] should concentrate on homework and club activities! Hi guys! I'm Nancy. I support (**the**)[25] school giving all students computers; then we wouldn't need (**the**)[26] lab! I also think the cafeteria should bring (**back**)[27] our favorite fried chicken. And school events need expanding. It's important for (**all**)[28] students to get together! Hey everybody! I'm Philip. First, I don't think there are enough events (**for**)[29] students. We should do more together! Next, (**we**)[30] should be able to use (**the**)[31] computer lab at the weekends, too. (**Also**)[32], vegans like me need more vegetable-only meals (**in**)[33] our cafeteria.

MET 2023 本 (4)

英語の音声を聞きながら，（　　）の中に，英単語を入れてください。

Today, our topic is the Asian elephant, the largest (　　　　)[1] animal in Asia. They are found across South and Southeast Asia. Asian elephants (　　　　)[2] sociable animals that usually live in groups and (　　　　)[3] known for helping each other. They are (　　　　)[4] intelligent and have the ability to (　　　　)[5] tools. The Asian elephant's population has dropped greatly over the (　　　　)[6] 75 years, even though this animal is listed as endangered. (　　　　)[7] has this happened? One reason for this decline (　　　　)[8] illegal human activities. Wild elephants have long been killed (　　　　)[9] ivory. But now, there is a developing market (　　　　)[10] other body parts, including skin and tail (　　　　)[11]. These body parts are used for accessories, (　　　　)[12] care products, and even medicine. Also, (　　　　)[13] number of wild elephants caught illegally is increasing because performing elephants are popular (　　　　)[14] tourist attractions. Housing developments and farming create other problems for elephants. Asian elephants need large areas to (　　　　)[15] in, but these human activities have reduced their natural habitats and created barriers between elephant groups. (　　　　)[16] a result, there is less contact between elephant groups and their numbers (　　　　)[17] declining. Also, many elephants are forced to (　　　　)[18] close to humans, resulting in deadly incidents for both humans (　　　　)[19] elephants. What actions have been taken to improve (　　　　)[20] Asian elephant's future? People are forming patrol units and other groups that watch for illegal activities. People (　　　　)[21] also making new routes to connect elephant habitats, and (　　　　)[22] constructing fences around local living areas to protect both people and elephants. Next, let's ( )^{23} at the current situation for elephants in different Asian countries. ( )^{24} group will give its report to ( )^{25} class. Our group studied deadly encounters between humans and elephants in Sri Lanka. In other countries,( )^{26} India, many more people than elephants die ( )^{27} these encounters. By contrast, similar efforts in Sri Lanka show a different trend. Let's ( )^{28} a look at the graph ( )^{29} the data we found.

問題英文の日本語訳を確認しよう。

今日のテーマは，アジアゾウです。アジア最大の陸上動物の。アジアゾウは南アジアと東南アジア全域で見られます。アジアゾウは社交的な動物で，普通は群れで生活し，互いに助け合うことで知られています。彼らは知能も高く，道具を使う能力もあります。アジアゾウは，過去75年間で個体数が大幅に減少しました。絶滅危惧種に指定されているにもかかわらず。なぜこのようなことが起きたのでしょうか？ この減少の理由の1つは，違法な人間の活動です。野生のゾウは長い間，殺されてきました。象牙のために。しかし現在では，新たな市場が発展しています。皮膚や尾毛など，他の体の部分の。これらの体の部分は，こんなことに使用されています。アクセサリー，スキンケア製品，さらには医薬品など。また，違法に捕獲される野生ゾウの数も増加しています。というのも，ゾウのパフォーマンスが人気があるからです。観光地での出し物として。住宅開発と農業はゾウにとって別の問題を引き起こします。アジアゾウが住むには広い面積が必要ですが，こうした人間の活動により自然の生息地が減少し，ゾウのグループ間に壁が生じています。その結果，ゾウの群れの間の接触が減り，ゾウの数が減少しています。また，多くのゾウは人間の近くで生活することを余儀なくされており，その結果，人間とゾウの両方に死亡事故が発生しています。どのような行動がとられてきたでしょうか？ アジアゾウの将来を改善するために。人々は，パトロール隊やその他のグループを結成しています。違法行為を監視するために。人々はまた，新しいルートを作り，ゾウの生息地を結ぼうとしています。また，地元の生活エリアの周囲に柵を建設しています。人とゾウの両方を守るために。次に，アジア各国のゾウの現状を見てみましょう。各グループがクラスの仲間に発表します。私たちのグループは，スリランカでの人間とゾウの致命的な遭遇を研究しました。インドなど他の国では，こういった致命的な遭遇の結果，ゾウよりもはるかに多くの人が命を落としています。対照的に，スリランカでの同様の取り組みは別の傾向を示しています。私たちが発見したグラフとデータを見てみましょう。

MET 2023 本 (4) 解答

解答付き英文を見ながら，英語の音声をもう一度聞いてみよう。

Today, our topic is the Asian elephant, the largest (**land**)[1] animal in Asia. They are found across South and Southeast Asia. Asian elephants (**are**)[2] sociable animals that usually live in groups and (**are**)[3] known for helping each other. They are (**also**)[4] intelligent and have the ability to (**use**)[5] tools. The Asian elephant's population has dropped greatly over the (**last**)[6] 75 years, even though this animal is listed as endangered. (**Why**)[7] has this happened? One reason for this decline (**is**)[8] illegal human activities. Wild elephants have long been killed (**for**)[9] ivory. But now, there is a developing market (**for**)[10] other body parts, including skin and tail (**hair**)[11]. These body parts are used for accessories, (**skin**)[12] care products, and even medicine. Also, (**the**)[13] number of wild elephants caught illegally is increasing because performing elephants are popular (**as**)[14] tourist attractions. Housing developments and farming create other problems for elephants. Asian elephants need large areas to (**live**)[15] in, but these human activities have reduced their natural habitats and created barriers between elephant groups. (**As**)[16] a result, there is less contact between elephant groups and their numbers (**are**)[17] declining. Also, many elephants are forced to (**live**)[18] close to humans, resulting in deadly incidents for both humans (**and**)[19] elephants. What actions have been taken to improve (**the**)[20] Asian elephant's future? People are forming patrol units and other groups that watch for illegal activities. People (**are**)[21] also making new routes to connect elephant habitats, and (**are**)[22] constructing fences around local living areas to protect both people and elephants. Next, let's (**look**)[23] at the current situation for elephants in different Asian countries. (**Each**)[24] group will give its report to (**the**)[25] class. Our group studied deadly encounters between humans and elephants in Sri Lanka. In other countries, (**like**)[26] India, many more people than elephants die (**in**)[27] these encounters. By contrast, similar efforts in Sri Lanka show a different trend. Let's (**take**)[28] a look at the graph (**and**)[29] the data we found.

MET 2023 本〔5〕

英語の音声を聞きながら，（　　）の中に，英単語を入れてください。

Hey, Mom! Let's go to Mt. Taka tomorrow. We've always wanted to go there. Well, I'm tired (　　　　)[1] work. I want to (　　　　)[2] home tomorrow. Oh, too bad. Can (　　　　)[3] go by myself, then? What? People always (　　　　)[4] you should never go hiking alone. What if (　　　　)[5] get lost? Yeah, I thought that (　　　　)[6] too, until I read a magazine article (　　　　)[7] solo hiking. Huh. What does the article (　　　　)[8] about it? It says it takes (　　　　)[9] time and effort to prepare for (　　　　)[10] hiking than group hiking. OK. But you can select (　　　　)[11] date that's convenient for you and (　　　　)[12] at your own pace. (　　　　)[13] imagine the sense of achievement once you're done, Mom! That's (　　　　)[14] good point. So, can I (　　　　)[15] up Mt. Taka by myself tomorrow? David, do you really (　　　　)[16] time to prepare for it? Well, (　　　　)[17] guess not. Why not wait until (　　　　)[18] weekend when you're ready? Then you can (　　　　)[19] on your own. OK, Mom.

Yay! We (　　　　)[20] got jobs downtown! I'm so relieved and excited. (　　　　)[21] said it, Mary! So, are (　　　　)[22] going to get a place near (　　　　)[23] office or in the suburbs? Oh, definitely close to (　　　　)[24] company. I'm not a morning person, so I (　　　　)[25] to be near the office. (　　　　)[26] should live near me, Lisa! Sorry, Mary. The (　　　　)[27] is too expensive. I want (　　　　)[28] save money. How about you, Kota? I'm with (　　　　)[29], Lisa. I don't mind waking up early and commuting (　　　　)[30] work by train. You know, while commuting (　　　　)[31] can listen to music. Oh, come on, ( )^{32} guys. We should enjoy the city life while we're young. There ( )^{33} so many things to do downtown. Jimmy's right. ( )^{34}, I want to get ( )^{35} dog. If I live ( )^{36} the office, I can get ( )^{37} earlier and take it for longer walks. Mary, don't ( )^{38} think your dog would be happier in ( )^{39} suburbs, where there's a lot more space? Yeah, you ( )^{40} be right, Lisa. Hmm, now I have ( )^{41} think again. Well, I want space for my training equipment. ( )^{42} wouldn't have that space in a ( )^{43} downtown apartment. That might be true for ( )^{44}, Kota. For me, a small apartment downtown is ( )^{45} fine. In fact, I've already found a ( )^{46} one. Great! When can we come over?

MET 2023 (5) 日本語訳

問題英文の日本語訳を確認しよう。

ねえ，お母さん！ 明日は鷹山に行こうよ。ずっとそこに行きたいと思ってるんだから。なんというか，仕事で疲れてるんだよねえ。明日は家にいたいな。困ったな。じゃあ，一人で行ってもいい？ えっ？ 一人でハイキングに行っちゃいけないって言われてるのよ。道に迷ったらどうするの？ そうだね，自分もそのこと考えてた。ソロハイキングに関する雑誌の記事を読むまでは。うん，じゃあ，その記事には何と書かれてるの？ ソロハイキングは，グループハイキングに比べて準備に時間と労力がかかるって。そうよねえ。でもね，ソロハイキングは，自分に都合の良い日を選んで，自分のペースで歩くことができるんだよ。そして，お母さん，それが終わったときの達成感を想像してみてよ！ それはいい点ね。じゃあ，明日は一人で鷹山にハイキングに行ってもいいでしょう？ デイビッド，本当に準備する時間があるの？ まあ，ないかもね。じゃあ，週末まで待ってみたら。準備が整うまで。そうすれば一人で行ってもいいよ。お母さん，分かったよ。

やったあ！ 私たち，皆，ダウンタウンで仕事見つけたよ！ 気楽になったし，わくわくするし。やったね，メアリー！ じゃあ，オフィスの近くに住む場所見つける，それとも郊外に住む？ ああ，会社の近くだね。朝型人間じゃないので，オフィスに近いところにいなきゃいけない。リサ，私の近くに住んでよ！ ごめんね，メアリー。家賃が高すぎ。お金を節約したいの。コウタはどう？ 私もリサと一緒だな。早起きして電車で通勤するの，別に苦じゃないし。あげくに，通勤中に音楽を聴くこともできる。あら，困っちゃうなあ。都会の生活を楽しんだ方がいいんじゃないの。若いうちに。ダウンタウンではやるべきことがたくさんあるじゃない。ジミーの言うとおりだね。あと，犬も飼いたいな。オフィスの近くに住んでれば，早く家に帰って，長い時間散歩に出かけられる。メアリー，あなたの犬は郊外のほうが幸せじゃない？ もっと広いスペースがある。そう，リサ，そうかもしれない。うーん，また考えなきゃいけない。そうねえ，トレーニング器具を置くスペースが欲しいな。ダウンタウンの小さなアパートには，そんなスペースないじゃない？ コウタ，それはあなたにも当てはまるかもね。私にとってはダウンタウンの小さなアパートで十分。実は，もういい物件を見つけちゃったんだ。すごい！ いつ行っていい？

MET 2023 本 (5) 解答

解答付き英文を見ながら，英語の音声をもう一度聞いてみよう。

Hey, Mom! Let's go to Mt. Taka tomorrow. We've always wanted to go there. Well, I'm tired (**from**)¹ work. I want to (**stay**)² home tomorrow. Oh, too bad. Can (**I**)³ go by myself, then? What? People always (**say**)⁴ you should never go hiking alone. What if (**you**)⁵ get lost? Yeah, I thought that (**way**)⁶ too, until I read a magazine article (**on**)⁷ solo hiking. Huh. What does the article (**say**)⁸ about it? It says it takes (**more**)⁹ time and effort to prepare for (**solo**)¹⁰ hiking than group hiking. OK. But you can select (**a**)¹¹ date that's convenient for you and (**walk**)¹² at your own pace. (**And**)¹³ imagine the sense of achievement once you're done, Mom! That's (**a**)¹⁴ good point. So, can I (**hike**)¹⁵ up Mt. Taka by myself tomorrow? David, do you really (**have**)¹⁶ time to prepare for it? Well, (**I**)¹⁷ guess not. Why not wait until (**next**)¹⁸ weekend when you're ready? Then you can (**go**)¹⁹ on your own. OK, Mom.

Yay! We (**all**)²⁰ got jobs downtown! I'm so relieved and excited. (**You**)²¹ said it, Mary! So, are (**you**)²² going to get a place near (**your**)²³ office or in the suburbs? Oh, definitely close to (**the**)²⁴ company. I'm not a morning person, so I (**need**)²⁵ to be near the office. (**You**)²⁶ should live near me, Lisa! Sorry, Mary. The (**rent**)²⁷ is too expensive. I want (**to**)²⁸ save money. How about you, Kota? I'm with (**you**)²⁹, Lisa. I don't mind waking up early and commuting (**to**)³⁰ work by train. You know, while commuting (**I**)³¹ can listen to music. Oh, come on, (**you**)³² guys. We should enjoy the city life while we're young. There (**are**)³³ so many things to do downtown. Jimmy's right. (**Also**)³⁴, I want to get (**a**)³⁵ dog. If I live (**near**)³⁶ the office, I can get (**home**)³⁷ earlier and take it for longer walks. Mary, don't (**you**)³⁸ think your dog would be happier in (**the**)³⁹ suburbs, where there's a lot more space? Yeah, you (**may**)⁴⁰ be right, Lisa. Hmm, now I have (**to**)⁴¹ think again. Well, I want space for my training equipment. (**I**)⁴² wouldn't have that space in a (**tiny**)⁴³ downtown apartment. That might be true for (**you**)⁴⁴, Kota. For me, a small apartment downtown is (**just**)⁴⁵ fine. In fact, I've already found a (**good**)⁴⁶ one. Great! When can we come over?

第2章

大学入学共通テスト追試験版 MET 問題

　この章には，問題が，15 題あります。全問題は，大学入学共通テスト英語追試験の聞き取りテストの過去問題の音声と英文を基に作られているので，MET 2021 追（1）のように，名前が付けられています。各問題には，空所（　）があります。音声を聞きながら，（　）の中に，英単語を入れて下さい。15 題は，5 題ずつ 3 つのグループに分かれ，3 つのグループは，進むにつれ，難度が上がっています。

　1 題終わるごとに，答え合わせをすることができます。各問題の次のページには，その英文の日本語訳が，そして，その次のページには，解答が太字で示されています。答え合わせが終わったら，問題のページに戻り，点数を記入しておくことができます。

MET 2021 追 (1)

／ 25 点

英語の音声を聞きながら，（　　）の中に，英単語を入れてください。

When does our club get together today? (　　　)[1] three? I'd like to wear a red tie (　　　)[2] work, but I only have blue (　　　)[3]. Would you tell me Kevin's email address, please? I (　　　)[4] Yoko's birthday cake, but I haven't finished wrapping her present yet. So I'll (　　　)[5] late for her party. This sign (　　　)[6] you can swim here, but you can't (　　　)[7] or barbecue. The chef is telling the waiter to (　　　)[8] both plates to the table. The park (　　　)[9] not as far from the station as (　　　)[10] café is. Can you take the cups (　　　)[11] the table and put the books (　　　)[12] instead? Done! Shall I close the window? Umm, leave (　　　)[13] open. Yeah, we need some fresh air. (　　　)[14] picture shows the room after the conversation? Let's stay (　　　)[15] the beach. But I'd rather be near the shopping (　　　)[16]. What about the hotel between the zoo (　　　)[17] the mall? Great, and it's across from the (　　　)[18]. Where will they stay? How about (　　　)[19] hamburger lunch? Actually, I'm trying to save money this month. Umm, perhaps (　　　)[20] chicken lunch is better, then. Well, I don't want salad, (　　　)[21] this one's perfect! Which meal will the man (　　　)[22] likely choose? Who's the boy with the dog, Ayaka? My nephew. (　　　)[23] to him is his twin sister. Is (　　　)[24] woman next to her your sister? No, she's my (　　　)[25], Tomo. Which person in the photo is Tomo?

MET 2021 追（1）日本語訳

問題英文の日本語訳を確認しよう。

私たちのクラブは今日いつ集まるの？　3時？　赤いネクタイをして仕事に行きたいんだけど，青い
ネクタイしか持ってないんだ。ケビンのメールアドレスを教えてくれない？　ヨウコのために，誕
生日ケーキを焼いたんだけど，プレゼント包むの，終わってないの。だから，パーティーに遅れる
わ。この標識を見ると，こんなことが書いてある。ここで泳ぐことはできるけど，キャンプやバー
ベキューはできないって。シェフはウェイターに皿を両方ともテーブルに持っていくように言って
る。公園は喫茶店ほど駅から遠くない。テーブルからカップを取って，代わりに本を置いてくれな
い？　できたよ！　窓を閉めようか？　うーん，開けたままにしといて。そうねえ，ちょっと空気入
れ替えた方がいいね。この会話の後の部屋の写真はどれですか？　ビーチの近くに泊まろう。私は，
ショッピングモールの近くがいいな。動物園とショッピングモールの間のホテルはどう？　いい
じゃない，公園の向かいだもんね。彼らはどこに滞在する予定ですか？　ハンバーグランチはどう？
実は，今月はお金を節約しようと思ってるの。うーん，それならチキンランチの方がいいかも。ま
あ，サラダはいらないので，これで完璧ね！　この男性は，どの食事を選ぶでしょう？　アヤカ，犬
を連れている男の子は誰？　私の甥。甥の隣が，その双子の妹。彼女の隣にいる女性はあなたの妹
ですか？　いいえ，私の叔母のトモです。写真の中の誰がトモですか？

MET 2021 追 (1) 解答

解答付き英文を見ながら，英語の音声をもう一度聞いてみよう。

When does our club get together today? (**At**)[1] three? I'd like to wear a red tie (**to**)[2] work, but I only have blue (**ones**)[3]. Would you tell me Kevin's email address, please? I (**baked**)[4] Yoko's birthday cake, but I haven't finished wrapping her present yet. So I'll (**be**)[5] late for her party. This sign (**says**)[6] you can swim here, but you can't (**camp**)[7] or barbecue. The chef is telling the waiter to (**take**)[8] both plates to the table. The park (**is**)[9] not as far from the station as (**the**)[10] café is. Can you take the cups (**off**)[11] the table and put the books (**there**)[12] instead? Done! Shall I close the window? Umm, leave (**it**)[13] open. Yeah, we need some fresh air. (**Which**)[14] picture shows the room after the conversation? Let's stay (**near**)[15] the beach. But I'd rather be near the shopping (**mall**)[16]. What about the hotel between the zoo (**and**)[17] the mall? Great, and it's across from the (**park**)[18]. Where will they stay? How about (**the**)[19] hamburger lunch? Actually, I'm trying to save money this month. Umm, perhaps (**the**)[20] chicken lunch is better, then. Well, I don't want salad, (**so**)[21] this one's perfect! Which meal will the man (**most**)[22] likely choose? Who's the boy with the dog, Ayaka? My nephew. (**Next**)[23] to him is his twin sister. Is (**the**)[24] woman next to her your sister? No, she's my (**aunt**)[25], Tomo. Which person in the photo is Tomo?

MET 2021 追 (2)

英語の音声を聞きながら，（　　）の中に，英単語を入れてください。

What would you like to do (　　　　)^1 graduation? Travel! But first I'm going to deliver newspapers until I (　　　　)^2 enough to go around the world. And you? (　　　　)^3 want to be a famous writer someday, but right (　　　　)^4, I need money, too. Maybe I (　　　　)^5 work for a magazine! Hey, Paul. I saw the (　　　　)^6 photo you posted on your blog yesterday. What? (　　　　)^7 posted that by mistake, but I thought I deleted it. No, (　　　　)^8 didn't. It's still on your blog. Are you serious, Karen? That's really embarrassing. (　　　　)^9 don't want people to see that photo of (　　　　)^{10}. I like both the blue one and (　　　　)^{11} black one. How about you? I see (　　　　)^{12} blue car, but where's the black one? Do (　　　　)^{13} mean that dark green one with the (　　　　)^{14} seats? Yes. Do you like that one? Well, it's OK, but (　　　　)^{15} like the other one better. You're Mike Smith, aren't you? Hey, Jane Adams, right? Yes! I haven't (　　　　)^{16} you for ages. Wasn't it five years ago, (　　　　)^{17} our class graduated? Yes, almost six. Well, I'm glad you recognized me. I haven't changed? No, (　　　　)^{18} recognized you immediately. You haven't changed your hairstyle at all. The textbook (　　　　)^{19} sold out at the bookstore. Do you (　　　　)^{20} where I can get one? Actually, I didn't buy (　　　　)^{21}. I got it from Peter. He took (　　　　)^{22} same course last year. So, who else (　　　　)^{23} that course? Alex! Yeah, but I know he gave (　　　　)^{24} book to his sister. Good morning. My flight's been cancelled. (　　　　)^{25} need to stay another night. Is there (　　　　)^{26} room available? Yes, but not until this afternoon. If (　　　　)^{27} come back later, we'll have one ready for (　　　　)^{28}. What time? About 3 o'clock? OK. I'll go out for (　　　　)^{29} and come back then.

MET 2021 追（2）日本語訳

問題英文の日本語訳を確認しよう。

卒業したら，何がしたい？ 旅！ でもまずは，新聞配達をするつもり。世界一周できるだけのお金が貯まるまで。君は？ いつか有名な作家になりたいんだけど，今はお金も必要。雑誌の仕事もできるかも！ やあ，ポール。面白い写真を見たよ。昨日君がブログに投稿したの。えっ？ 間違えて投稿したんだけど，消したと思ってたよ。いや，消えてないよ。まだブログに載ってるよ。カレン，本気で言ってる？ いや，本当に恥ずかしいな。その写真，人に見られたくないなあ。青いのも黒いのも，どちらも好きだなあ。あなたは？ 青い車は見えるけど，黒い車はどこ？ 濃い緑色の車のこと？ 白いシートの。そうそう。あれ，好き？ まあ，いいと思うけど，もう一方の方が好きだな。マイク・スミスだよね？ ジェーン・アダムス，だね？ そうそう！ もう何年も会ってなかったねえ。もう5年も前じゃない？ 卒業したの。そうそう，ほぼ6年だね。なんというか，私だと分かってくれて嬉しいよ。変わってなかった？ ぜんぜん，すぐ分かったよ。髪型をまったく変えてなかったね。その教科書は本屋で売り切れ。どこで入手できるか知ってる？ 実は，私，購入してないの。ピーターからもらったんだ。ピーターは昨年同じコースを取ってたの。じゃあ，他にそのコースを取ってた人は誰かなあ？ アレックス！ そうそう，でもアレックスは，自分の妹にあげたんだよね。おはよう。フライトがキャンセルされまして。もう一泊する必要があるんです。空室はありますか？ はい，でも今日の午後まではございません。後で戻ってきていただければ，ご用意させていただきます。何時ですか？ 3時くらいでどうでしょうか？ わかりました。お昼ご飯を食べに行って，また戻ってきます。

MET 2021 追（2）解答

解答付き英文を見ながら，英語の音声をもう一度聞いてみよう。

What would you like to do (**after**)¹ graduation? Travel! But first I'm going to deliver newspapers until I (**save**)² enough to go around the world. And you? (**I**)³ want to be a famous writer someday, but right (**now**)⁴, I need money, too. Maybe I (**can**)⁵ work for a magazine! Hey, Paul. I saw the (**funny**)⁶ photo you posted on your blog yesterday. What? (**I**)⁷ posted that by mistake, but I thought I deleted it. No, (**you**)⁸ didn't. It's still on your blog. Are you serious, Karen? That's really embarrassing. (**I**)⁹ don't want people to see that photo of (**me**)¹⁰. I like both the blue one and (**the**)¹¹ black one. How about you? I see (**the**)¹² blue car, but where's the black one? Do (**you**)¹³ mean that dark green one with the (**white**)¹⁴ seats? Yes. Do you like that one? Well, it's OK, but (**I**)¹⁵ like the other one better. You're Mike Smith, aren't you? Hey, Jane Adams, right? Yes! I haven't (**seen**)¹⁶ you for ages. Wasn't it five years ago, (**when**)¹⁷ our class graduated? Yes, almost six. Well, I'm glad you recognized me. I haven't changed? No, (**I**)¹⁸ recognized you immediately. You haven't changed your hairstyle at all. The textbook (**is**)¹⁹ sold out at the bookstore. Do you (**know**)²⁰ where I can get one? Actually, I didn't buy (**mine**)²¹. I got it from Peter. He took (**the**)²² same course last year. So, who else (**took**)²³ that course? Alex! Yeah, but I know he gave (**his**)²⁴ book to his sister. Good morning. My flight's been cancelled. (**I**)²⁵ need to stay another night. Is there (**a**)²⁶ room available? Yes, but not until this afternoon. If (**you**)²⁷ come back later, we'll have one ready for (**you**)²⁸. What time? About 3 o'clock? OK. I'll go out for (**lunch**)²⁹ and come back then.

英語の音声を聞きながら，（　　）の中に，英単語を入れてください。

Here are the average summer and winter temperatures of four cities in North America: Columbus, Hopeville, Lansfield, (　　　　)[1] Rockport. The temperature of Lansfield in the summer was much higher (　　　　)[2] I expected—the highest in fact. By comparison, Rockport had (　　　)[3] much cooler summer than Lansfield and experienced the coldest winter among the four cities. Columbus (　　　　)[4] a bit cooler than Rockport in the summer, while (　　　)[5] winter was a few degrees warmer. Hopeville changed the least in temperature (　　　　)[6] was just a bit cooler than Lansfield in (　　　)[7] summer. Attention, please! There are some changes to the regular bus schedule. (　　　　)[8] A2 bus leaving for City Center is canceled. Those passengers going to City Center should (　　　)[9] take the C10 bus to Main Street. It'll continue on to City Center (　　　)[10] leaving Main Street, which takes 10 additional minutes. The A6 bus, which goes (　　　　)[11] City Center, is running normally. Finally, the B7 bus to Eastern Avenue will leave (　　　　)[12] an hour late. We're sorry for any inconvenience.

(　　　　)[13] hotel's internship focuses on creating a new website. The work will (　　　)[14] done in late August. Interns will help set (　　　)[15] the website, which should take about half a (　　　　)[16]. You can stay at our hotel (　　　　)[17] come from home. The internship at our language school starts (　　　　)[18] early summer when the exchange program starts. Many international students visit us, (　　　　)[19] we need to help these students get around. Interns should ( )[20] at the dormitory for about ten days while assisting ( )[21] the program. Public library interns help with our reading programs. For example, they prepare ( )[22] special events and put returned books back on the shelves. Interns ( )[23] work for more than two weeks. You ( )[24] join anytime during the summer, and housing is available. We're a software company looking for students ( )[25] help develop a smartphone application. They are required to participate in brainstorming sessions, starting ( )[26] the 15th of July, and are expected to stay ( )[27] the end of August. Participants should find their own ( )[28] to stay.

問題英文の日本語訳を確認しよう。

ここに，北米の4つの都市の夏と冬の平均気温が示してある。コロンバス，ホープビル，ランズフィールド，ロックポートの4都市。夏のランズフィールドの気温は予想よりもはるかに高く，実際最高だった。比較すると，ロックポートはランズフィールドよりも夏がずっと涼しく，冬は4つの都市の中で最も寒かった。コロンバスは夏はロックポートよりも少し涼しかったが，冬は数度暖かかった。ホープビルは気温の変化が最も少なく，夏はランズフィールドよりもほんの少し涼しかった。ご注意ください！ 定期バスの時刻表に一部変更がございます。市内中心部行きの A2 バスは欠航となっております。市内中心部に行く乗客は，メインストリート行きの C10 バスにご乗車ください。メインストリートを出て市内中心部まで進みますが，さらに 10 分かかります。市内中心部行きの A6 バスは通常通り運行しております。最後に，Eastern Avenue 行きの B7 バスは30 分遅れで出発します。ご不便をおかけして申し訳ございません。

当ホテルのインターンシップは，新しいウェブサイトの作成に焦点を当てています。この作業は8月下旬に終了します。インターン生はウェブサイトの立ち上げを手伝いますが，これには半月程度かかります。当ホテルにご宿泊いただくことも，ご自宅からお越しいただくことも可能です。私たちの語学学校でのインターンシップは，交換留学プログラムが始まる初夏に始まります。多くの留学生が来校するため，留学生があちこち見て回るのをサポートする必要があります。インターン生は寮に 10 日間程度滞在してプログラムの手伝いをします。公共図書館のインターン生が読書プログラムを手伝ってくれます。例えば，特別なイベントの準備をしたり，返却された本を本棚に戻したりします。インターン生は 2 週間以上働く必要があります。夏の間はいつでも参加でき，住居も用意されています。私たちはソフトウェア会社で，スマートフォンアプリの開発を手伝ってくれる学生を募集しています。参加学生は，ブレインストーミングセッション，7 月 15 日に始まりますが，それに参加し，8 月末まで滞在することになっています。参加者は，各自，宿泊場所を見つけてください。

MET 2021 追（3）解答

解答付き英文を見ながら，英語の音声をもう一度聞いてみよう。

Here are the average summer and winter temperatures of four cities in North America: Columbus, Hopeville, Lansfield, (**and**)¹ Rockport. The temperature of Lansfield in the summer was much higher (**than**)² I expected—the highest in fact. By comparison, Rockport had (**a**)³ much cooler summer than Lansfield and experienced the coldest winter among the four cities. Columbus (**was**)⁴ a bit cooler than Rockport in the summer, while (**its**)⁵ winter was a few degrees warmer. Hopeville changed the least in temperature (**and**)⁶ was just a bit cooler than Lansfield in (**the**)⁷ summer. Attention, please! There are some changes to the regular bus schedule. (**The**)⁸ A2 bus leaving for City Center is canceled. Those passengers going to City Center should (**now**)⁹ take the C10 bus to Main Street. It'll continue on to City Center (**after**)¹⁰ leaving Main Street, which takes 10 additional minutes. The A6 bus, which goes (**to**)¹¹ City Center, is running normally. Finally, the B7 bus to Eastern Avenue will leave (**half**)¹² an hour late. We're sorry for any inconvenience.

(**Our**)¹³ hotel's internship focuses on creating a new website. The work will (**be**)¹⁴ done in late August. Interns will help set (**up**)¹⁵ the website, which should take about half a (**month**)¹⁶. You can stay at our hotel (**or**)¹⁷ come from home. The internship at our language school starts (**in**)¹⁸ early summer when the exchange program starts. Many international students visit us, (**so**)¹⁹ we need to help these students get around. Interns should (**stay**)²⁰ at the dormitory for about ten days while assisting (**with**)²¹ the program. Public library interns help with our reading programs. For example, they prepare (**for**)²² special events and put returned books back on the shelves. Interns (**must**)²³ work for more than two weeks. You (**can**)²⁴ join anytime during the summer, and housing is available. We're a software company looking for students (**to**)²⁵ help develop a smartphone application. They are required to participate in brainstorming sessions, starting (**on**)²⁶ the 15th of July, and are expected to stay (**until**)²⁷ the end of August. Participants should find their own (**place**)²⁸ to stay.

MET 2021 追 (4)

英語の音声を聞きながら，(　　) の中に，英単語を入れてください。

OK. What is blue carbon? You know, humans produce too (　　　　)[1] CO_2, a greenhouse gas. This creates problems with the earth's climate. But remember (　　　　)[2] trees help us by absorbing CO_2 from the (　　　　)[3] and releasing oxygen? Trees change CO_2 into organic carbon, which is stored in biomass. Biomass includes things (　　　　)[4] leaves and trunks. The organic carbon in the biomass then goes (　　　　)[5] the soil. This organic carbon is called "green" carbon. But listen! Plants growing on (　　　　)[6] coasts can also take in and store CO_2 (　　　　)[7] organic carbon in biomass and soil—just like trees (　　　　)[8] dry land do. That's called "blue" carbon. Blue carbon is created by seagrasses, mangroves, (　　　　)[9] plants in saltwater wetlands. These blue carbon ecosystems cover much less surface (　　　　)[10] the earth than is covered by green carbon forests. However, (　　　　)[11] store carbon very efficiently—much more carbon per hectare than (　　　　)[12] carbon forests do. The carbon in the soil of (　　　　)[13] ocean floor is covered by layers of mud, (　　　　)[14] can stay there for millions of years. (　　　　)[15] contrast, the carbon in land soil is so (　　　　)[16] to the surface that it can easily mix (　　　　)[17] air, and then be released as CO_2. Currently the (　　　　)[18] carbon ecosystem is in trouble. For this ecosystem to work, (　　　　)[19] is absolutely necessary to look after ocean coasts. For example, (　　　　)[20] areas of mangroves are being destroyed. When this happens, (　　　　)[21] amounts of blue carbon are released back into the atmosphere (　　　　)[22] CO_2. To avoid this, ocean coasts must be restored (　　　　)[23] protected.

Additionally, healthy coastline ecosystems will support fish life, giving us even more benefits. (   )[24] at this graph, which compares blue and (   )[25] carbon storage. Notice how much organic carbon is stored in each of (   )[26] four places. The organic carbon is stored in soil and in biomass (   )[27] in different proportions. What can we learn from (   )[28]?

問題英文の日本語訳を確認しよう。

さて。ブルーカーボンとは何でしょうか？ ご存知のように，人間は CO_2 を過剰に生成します。温室効果ガスのことです。これは地球の気候に問題を引き起こします。しかし，樹木が私たちをどのように助けているかわかりますか？ 空気から CO_2 を吸収し，酸素を放出することで。樹木は CO_2 を有機炭素に変え，それは，バイオマスに貯蔵されます。バイオマスには葉や幹などが含まれます。バイオマス中の有機炭素は土壌に入ります。この有機炭素は「グリーン」カーボンと呼ばれます。でも聞いてください！ 海岸で生育する植物も，CO_2 を有機炭素としてバイオマスや土壌に取り込み，貯蔵することができます。陸地の樹木と同じように。それは「ブルー」カーボンと呼ばれます。ブルーカーボンは，海草，マングローブ，海水湿地の植物によって作られます。これらのブルーカーボン生態系がカバーする地球の表面は，グリーンカーボン森林がカバーする面積よりもはるかに少ないです。しかし，それらは非常に効率的に炭素を貯蔵し，グリーンカーボン森林よりもヘクタールあたりはるかに多くの炭素を貯蔵します。海底の土壌中の炭素は泥の層で覆われており，何百万年もそこに留まることができます。対照的に，陸上土壌中の炭素は地表に非常に近いため，空気と容易に混合し，その後 CO_2 として放出されます。現在，ブルーカーボン生態系は困難に直面しています。この生態系が機能するためには，海岸をよく保つことが絶対的に必要です。例えば，広範囲のマングローブ林が破壊されています。これが起こると，大量のブルーカーボンが CO_2 として大気中に放出されます。これを避けるためには，海岸を回復させ，保護する必要があります。さらに，健全な海岸線の生態系は魚の生息をサポートし，私たちにさらに多くの恩恵をもたらします。このグラフを見てください。ブルーカーボンとグリーンカーボンの貯蔵量を比較したものです。注目していただきたいのは，どれだけ有機炭素がこの4つの場所にそれぞれ貯蔵されているかです。有機炭素は土壌およびバイオマスに貯蔵されますが，その割合は異なります。このことから何が学べるでしょうか？

MET 2021 追 (4) 解答

解答付き英文を見ながら，英語の音声をもう一度聞いてみよう。

OK. What is blue carbon? You know, humans produce too (**much**)[1] CO_2, a greenhouse gas. This creates problems with the earth's climate. But remember (**how**)[2] trees help us by absorbing CO_2 from the (**air**)[3] and releasing oxygen? Trees change CO_2 into organic carbon, which is stored in biomass. Biomass includes things (**like**)[4] leaves and trunks. The organic carbon in the biomass then goes (**into**)[5] the soil. This organic carbon is called "green" carbon. But listen! Plants growing on (**ocean**)[6] coasts can also take in and store CO_2 (**as**)[7] organic carbon in biomass and soil— just like trees (**on**)[8] dry land do. That's called "blue" carbon. Blue carbon is created by seagrasses, mangroves, (**and**)[9] plants in saltwater wetlands. These blue carbon ecosystems cover much less surface (**of**)[10] the earth than is covered by green carbon forests. However, (**they**)[11] store carbon very efficiently—much more carbon per hectare than (**green**)[12] carbon forests do. The carbon in the soil of (**the**)[13] ocean floor is covered by layers of mud, (**and**)[14] can stay there for millions of years. (**In**)[15] contrast, the carbon in land soil is so (**close**)[16] to the surface that it can easily mix (**with**)[17] air, and then be released as CO_2. Currently the (**blue**)[18] carbon ecosystem is in trouble. For this ecosystem to work, (**it**)[19] is absolutely necessary to look after ocean coasts. For example, (**large**)[20] areas of mangroves are being destroyed. When this happens, (**great**)[21] amounts of blue carbon are released back into the atmosphere (**as**)[22] CO_2. To avoid this, ocean coasts must be restored (**and**)[23] protected. Additionally, healthy coastline ecosystems will support fish life, giving us even more benefits. (**Look**)[24] at this graph, which compares blue and (**green**)[25] carbon storage. Notice how much organic carbon is stored in each of (**the**)[26] four places. The organic carbon is stored in soil and in biomass (**but**)[27] in different proportions. What can we learn from (**this**)[28]?

英語の音声を聞きながら，（　　）の中に，英単語を入れてください。

What are you doing, Bob? I'm writing a letter to (　　　　)[1] grandmother. Nice paper! But isn't it easier just to (　　　　)[2] her an email? Well, perhaps. But I like shopping (　　　　)[3] stationery, putting pen to paper, addressing the envelope, and going (　　　　)[4] the post office. It gives me time (　　　　)[5] think about my grandma. Uh-huh. But that's so much trouble. (　　　　)[6] really. Don't you think your personality shines through in a handwritten letter? And (　　　　)[7] makes people happy. Plus, it has cognitive benefits. What cognitive benefits? (　　　　)[8] know, handwriting is good for thinking processes, like memorizing and decision making. Really? I'm (　　　　)[9] more fluent writer when I do it on (　　　　)[10] computer. Maybe you are, but you might (　　　　)[11] sacrifice something with that efficiency. Like what? Well, mindfulness, for one. Mindfulness? Like taking (　　　　)[12] to do things with careful consideration. That's being lost these (　　　　)[13]. We should slow down and lead a (　　　　)[14] mindful life. Speaking of mindful, I wouldn't mind some chocolate-chip ice (　　　　)[15]. Hey, Kenji. Did you vote yet? The polls (　　　　)[16] in two hours. Well, Brad, who should I vote for? (　　　　)[17] don't know about politics. Seriously? You should be more politically aware. (　　　　)[18] don't know. It's hard. How can I make (　　　　)[19] educated choice? What do you think, Alice? The information is everywhere, Kenji! (　　　　)[20] go online. Many young people are doing it. Really, Alice? (　　　　)[21]? Either way, you should take more interest in elections. Is everybody(　　　　)[22] that? There's Helen. Let's ask her.

Hey Helen! Hello, Kenji. What's up? Are you (   )^{23} to vote? Vote? We're only twenty. Most people our (   )^{24} don't care about politics. Being young is no excuse. (   )^{25} unlike older people, I'm just not interested. Come on, Helen. Let's just (   )^{26}. That might change your mind. Brad's right. Talking with friends (   )^{27} you informed. Really? Would that help? It might, Kenji. (   )^{28} can learn about politics that way. So, Kenji, (   )^{29} you going to vote or not? (   )^{30} my one vote meaningful? Every vote counts, Kenji. I'll worry about voting (   )^{31} I'm old. But do what you want! OK, I'm convinced. We've (   )^{32} two hours. Let's figure out who to vote for!

MET 2021 追（5）日本語訳

問題英文の日本語訳を確認しよう。

ボブ，何してるの？ 祖母に手紙を書いてるんだ。素敵な便箋ね！ でも，メールの方が簡単じゃないの？ まあ，そうだろうねえ。でも，文房具を買ったり，手書きをしたり，封筒に宛名を書いたり，郵便局に行ったりするのが好きなんだ。祖母のことを考える時間もできるし。そうね。でもけっこう面倒じゃない？ そうでもないよ。手書きの手紙には，人の個性が表れるって思わない？ あげくに，人をいい気分にさせると思うよ。さらには，脳にとってのメリットもあるし。どんなメリット？ 手書きは，思考プロセスにいいんだよ。記憶や意思決定みたいな。本当？ コンピューターなら，上手に書ける方なんだけどなあ。きっとそうだと思うけど，でも，その効率化のために何かを犠牲にしてるかもね。どんな？ そうだねえ，1つあげるとすれば，マインドフルネスってものかな。マインドフルネス？ 時間をかけて慎重に物事を行うってこと。それが最近は失われつつあるよね。ペースを落として，もっとマインドフルな生活を送ってもいいんじゃない？ マインドフルといえば，チョコチップアイスクリーム，出してもらっても構いませんけど。やあ，ケンジ。もう投票した？ 投票は2時間後に終わるよ。ねえ，ブラッド，誰に投票したらいい？ 政治のこと，ぜんぜん分からないんだよ。本気で言ってる？ もっと政治を気にかけないと。わかんない。難しい。どうやったら，賢く選べるの？ アリス，どう思う？ ケンジ，情報はどこにでもあるのよ！ ネット見て。若者はみんなそうしてるよ。アリス，本当？ みんな？ なんでもいいけど，選挙にもっと関心を持ったほうがいいね。みんなそうなの？ ヘレンがいるよ。彼女に聞いてみようよ。やあ，ヘレン！ こんにちは，ケンジ。どうしたの？ 投票するの？ 投票？ まだ二十歳だよ。私たちの年齢のほとんどの人は政治に興味なんてないよ。若いということは言い訳にはならないよ。でも，年上の人と違って，私はまったく興味がないのよ。困ったなあ，ヘレン。ちょっと話そう。そうすれば気が変わるかもしれないから。ブラッドの言うとおり。友達と話せば，情報が得られるよ。本当？ 役に立つかな？ ケンジ，立つかもよ。こうやって政治について学べるんじゃない？ それで，ケンジ，投票するの，しないの？ 自分の一票って，意味あるのかなあ？ ケンジ，どの一票も大切なんだ。投票のことを気に掛けるよ，年を取ったら。でも，やりたいことはやろう！ わかったよ。納得。まだ2時間ある。誰に投票するか考えてみよう！

MET 2021 追（5）解答

解答付き英文を見ながら，英語の音声をもう一度聞いてみよう。

What are you doing, Bob? I'm writing a letter to（ **my** ）[1] grandmother. Nice paper! But isn't it easier just to（ **write** ）[2] her an email? Well, perhaps. But I like shopping（ **for** ）[3] stationery, putting pen to paper, addressing the envelope, and going（ **to** ）[4] the post office. It gives me time（ **to** ）[5] think about my grandma. Uh-huh. But that's so much trouble. （ **Not** ）[6] really. Don't you think your personality shines through in a handwritten letter? And（ **it** ）[7] makes people happy. Plus, it has cognitive benefits. What cognitive benefits? （ **You** ）[8] know, handwriting is good for thinking processes, like memorizing and decision making. Really? I'm（ **a** ）[9] more fluent writer when I do it on（ **a** ）[10] computer. Maybe you are, but you might（ **also** ）[11] sacrifice something with that efficiency. Like what? Well, mindfulness, for one. Mindfulness? Like taking（ **time** ）[12] to do things with careful consideration. That's being lost these（ **days** ）[13]. We should slow down and lead a （ **more** ）[14] mindful life. Speaking of mindful, I wouldn't mind some chocolate-chip ice （ **cream** ）[15]. Hey, Kenji. Did you vote yet? The polls（ **close** ）[16] in two hours. Well, Brad, who should I vote for? （ **I** ）[17] don't know about politics. Seriously? You should be more politically aware. （ **I** ）[18] don't know. It's hard. How can I make（ **an** ）[19] educated choice? What do you think, Alice? The information is everywhere, Kenji! （ **Just** ）[20] go online. Many young people are doing it. Really, Alice? （ **Many** ）[21]? Either way, you should take more interest in elections. Is everybody（ **like** ）[22] that? There's Helen. Let's ask her. Hey Helen! Hello, Kenji. What's up? Are you（ **going** ）[23] to vote? Vote? We're only twenty. Most people our（ **age** ）[24] don't care about politics. Being young is no excuse. （ **But** ）[25] unlike older people, I'm just not interested. Come on, Helen. Let's just（ **talk** ）[26]. That might change your mind. Brad's right. Talking with friends （ **keeps** ）[27] you informed. Really? Would that help? It might, Kenji. （ **We** ）[28] can learn about politics that way. So, Kenji, （ **are** ）[29] you going to vote or not? （ **Is** ）[30] my one vote meaningful? Every vote counts, Kenji. I'll worry about voting（ **when** ）[31] I'm old. But do what you want! OK, I'm convinced. We've（ **got** ）[32] two hours. Let's figure out who to vote for!

MET 2022 追（1）

／27 点

英語の音声を聞きながら，（　）の中に，英単語を入れてください。

Have you finished your homework? I've already done mine. I'm (　　　　)[1], Meg. Do you mind if I (　　　　)[2] home? Hello? Oh, Jill. Can I call you (　　　　)[3]? I have to get on (　　　　)[4] train right now. We have (　　　　)[5] bread and milk, but there aren't (　　　　)[6] eggs. I'll go and buy some. (　　　　)[7] books are next to the flowers, (　　　　)[8] the clock. The hotel is taller (　　　　)[9] the hospital, but the tree is (　　　　)[10] tallest. Oh, we can't get a table. They're full. Well, (　　　　)[11] glove I lost is white. (　　　　)[12] you describe it more? There's a heart, oh... no, three (　　　　)[13] them, and a button. It's here. Please come (　　　　)[14] get it. Which one is her (　　　　)[15] glove? Will you just use (　　　　)[16] in your room? No, sometimes I'll take it outside. (　　　　)[17], how about this square one? Cool. And (　　　　)[18] tells the time, too. Which one (　　　　)[19] the woman buy? Nice coat. Thanks. It's (　　　　)[20] and goes well with these (　　　　)[21]. But it's so warm today. OK, I'll wear (　　　　)[22] instead. But I'll keep this on. Bye. How (　　　　)[23] the sister dressed when she goes out? Didn't (　　　　)[24] park the car on Level 6? Not 7? No! You're (　　　　)[25]. It was next to Elevator A. Yeah, we walked directly across (　　　　)[26] bridge into the store. Where did (　　　　)[27] park their car?

MET 2022 追（1）日本語訳

問題英文の日本語訳を確認しよう。

宿題はもう終わった？　自分のはもう終わったよ。メグ，疲れたよ。家に帰ってもいいかな？　もしもし？　ああ，ジル。折り返し電話してもいい？　今すぐ電車に乗らなきゃならないの。パンと牛乳はあるんだけど，卵がないんだよ。行って買ってくるよ。本は花の隣，時計の下にある。ホテルは病院より高いが，木が一番高い。ああ，テーブルが予約できない。いっぱいだって。あのー，私が失くした手袋は白色なんです。もっと詳しく説明してもらえますか？　ハートが3つあって，ボタンが1つあります。ここにありますよ。取りに来てください。彼女が失くした手袋はどれですか？自分の部屋だけで使う？　いや，たまには外に持ち出しますよ。では，この四角いのはどう？　いいね。時間も知らせてくれるし。この女性はどれを買うでしょうか？　素敵なコート。ありがとう。新しくて，このブーツとよく合うと思うんだ。でも今日はけっこう暖かいよね。そうね，代わりにこれを履いていこうかな。でも，このコートは着ていくよ。じゃあね。この妹は外出するときどんな服装をしていますか。6階に車を停めなかったっけ？　7階じゃなかった？　いや！　あなたが正しい。エレベーター A の隣にあったよ。そうそう，橋を渡って直接お店に入ったよね。彼らは車をどこに駐車しましたか？

MET 2022 追（1）解答

解答付き英文を見ながら，英語の音声をもう一度聞いてみよう。

Have you finished your homework? I've already done mine. I'm (**tired**)[1], Meg. Do you mind if I (**go**)[2] home? Hello? Oh, Jill. Can I call you (**back**)[3]? I have to get on (**the**)[4] train right now. We have (**some**)[5] bread and milk, but there aren't (**any**)[6] eggs. I'll go and buy some. (**The**)[7] books are next to the flowers, (**below**)[8] the clock. The hotel is taller (**than**)[9] the hospital, but the tree is (**the**)[10] tallest. Oh, we can't get a table. They're full. Well, (**the**)[11] glove I lost is white. (**Can**)[12] you describe it more? There's a heart, oh... no, three (**of**)[13] them, and a button. It's here. Please come (**and**)[14] get it. Which one is her (**lost**)[15] glove? Will you just use (**it**)[16] in your room? No, sometimes I'll take it outside. (**So**)[17], how about this square one? Cool. And (**it**)[18] tells the time, too. Which one (**will**)[19] the woman buy? Nice coat. Thanks. It's (**new**)[20] and goes well with these (**boots**)[21]. But it's so warm today. OK, I'll wear (**these**)[22] instead. But I'll keep this on. Bye. How (**is**)[23] the sister dressed when she goes out? Didn't (**we**)[24] park the car on Level 6? Not 7? No! You're (**right**)[25]. It was next to Elevator A. Yeah, we walked directly across (**the**)[26] bridge into the store. Where did (**they**)[27] park their car?

MET 2022 追 (2)

／34 点

英語の音声を聞きながら，（　　）の中に，英単語を入れてください。

Excuse me. Do you have time (　　　　)[1] a short interview? What's it about? We're doing research (　　　　)[2] how people deal with stress. That's interesting! I'm really busy, but (　　　　)[3] can spare a couple of minutes. How (　　　　)[4] will it take? It should take (　　　　)[5] 10 minutes. Oh, sorry. Let's all get together next weekend. Sure! I'm (　　　　)[6] on Saturday, but Sunday would be fine. (　　　　)[7] about Mom and Dad? Mom says either day is OK, (　　　　)[8] Dad is only free on Saturday. I (　　　　)[9].... Why don't you go ahead without me? I'll (　　　　)[10] next time! Oh well, OK. I didn't know you (　　　　)[11] working at the convenience store. Yes, I used (　　　　)[12] work there every day, but (　　　　)[13] just three times a week, on weekdays. (　　　　)[14] you working anywhere else besides that? Yes, at the café (　　　　)[15] the station, two days, every weekend. Wow! You're working a lot! (　　　　)[16] happened? Where did you go? I (　　　　)[17] lost and ended up in (　　　　)[18] rose garden. So, you decided to come straight (　　　　)[19] then? Well, no. First, I tried to (　　　　)[20] you. Why didn't you call me? (　　　　)[21] didn't have my phone. But I (　　　　)[22] OK. The flowers were nice. Do you (　　　　)[23] to eat dinner after work? I (　　　　)[24] so, but where? The sushi place across (　　　　)[25] the office? Not there again! Let's get (　　　　)[26] from the office. OK... what about the Italian restaurant (　　　　)[27] the station, then? That's far! Is it? It's (　　　　)[28] your way home! Yeah, OK. You took (　　　　)[29] 7:30 train this morning, right? Yes. Did you (　　　　)[30] me at the station? No, I saw (　　　　)[31] on the train. I took (　　　　)[32] train, too. Why didn't you say (　　　　)[33]? Weren't you talking with somebody? No, I was alone. Really? (　　　　)[34] must've been someone else, then.

MET 2022 追（2）日本語訳

問題英文の日本語訳を確認しよう。

すみません。ちょっとインタビュー，よろしいですか？ 何の？ 人がストレスにどう対処するか調査しているんです。おもしろそうね！ 実は忙しいんだけど，数分なら大丈夫よ。どのくらい時間かかるの？ だいたい 10 分です。あら，ごめんなさい。来週末，みんなで集まろうよ。もちろん！ 土曜日は忙しいけど，日曜日なら大丈夫。お父さんとお母さんはどう？ お母さんはどちらでもいいって言ってるけど，お父さんは土曜日しか空いてないって。そうかあ。じゃあ，私なしで先に進めてくれない？ 次回は来るから！ そうね，わかったわ。コンビニで働いているとは知らなかったよ。そう，以前は毎日そこで働いていたんだけど，今は平日に週 3 日だけ。それ以外にどこかで働いてるの？ そう，駅の近くのカフェで，毎週末 2 日。あらあ！ けっこう働いてるねえ！ どうしたの？ どこに行ったの？ 道に迷って，結局，バラ園に着いちゃった。それで，そのまま家に帰ることにしたの？ うーん，ちょっと違うかな。まず，あなたを見つけようとしたのよ。なぜ電話してくれなかったの？ 電話を持ってなかったのよ。でも大丈夫だったわよ。花も素敵だったしね。仕事の後に晩御飯しない？ いいわねえ，どこで？ オフィスの向かいの寿司屋？ そこは，ないわ！ オフィスから離れたところで。そうね，じゃあ，駅の近くのイタリアンはどう？ ちょっと遠いなあ！ そう？ あなたの家の方よ！ そうね，じゃあ，そこで。今朝 7 時半の電車に乗ったよね？ ええ。駅で私を見なかった？ いえ，列車の中で見かけたよ。私もその電車に乗ってたから。じゃあなぜ一声掛けてくれなかったの？ 誰かと話してなかった？ いえ，一人だったわよ。本当に？ じゃあ，別人だったのかなあ。

MET 2022 追（2）解答

解答付き英文を見ながら，英語の音声をもう一度聞いてみよう。

Excuse me. Do you have time (**for**)[1] a short interview? What's it about? We're doing research (**on**)[2] how people deal with stress. That's interesting! I'm really busy, but (**I**)[3] can spare a couple of minutes. How (**long**)[4] will it take? It should take (**about**)[5] 10 minutes. Oh, sorry. Let's all get together next weekend. Sure! I'm (**busy**)[6] on Saturday, but Sunday would be fine. (**How**)[7] about Mom and Dad? Mom says either day is OK, (**but**)[8] Dad is only free on Saturday. I (**see**)[9].... Why don't you go ahead without me? I'll (**come**)[10] next time! Oh well, OK. I didn't know you (**were**)[11] working at the convenience store. Yes, I used (**to**)[12] work there every day, but (**now**)[13] just three times a week, on weekdays. (**Are**)[14] you working anywhere else besides that? Yes, at the café (**near**)[15] the station, two days, every weekend. Wow! You're working a lot! (**What**)[16] happened? Where did you go? I (**got**)[17] lost and ended up in (**the**)[18] rose garden. So, you decided to come straight (**home**)[19] then? Well, no. First, I tried to (**find**)[20] you. Why didn't you call me? (**I**)[21] didn't have my phone. But I (**was**)[22] OK. The flowers were nice. Do you (**want**)[23] to eat dinner after work? I (**guess**)[24] so, but where? The sushi place across (**from**)[25] the office? Not there again! Let's get (**away**)[26] from the office. OK... what about the Italian restaurant (**near**)[27] the station, then? That's far! Is it? It's (**on**)[28] your way home! Yeah, OK. You took (**the**)[29] 7:30 train this morning, right? Yes. Did you (**see**)[30] me at the station? No, I saw (**you**)[31] on the train. I took (**that**)[32] train, too. Why didn't you say (**hello**)[33]? Weren't you talking with somebody? No, I was alone. Really? (**That**)[34] must've been someone else, then.

MET 2022 追 (3)

英語の音声を聞きながら，（　　）の中に，英単語を入れてください。

Let's review the schedule for Parents' Day. The event will (　　　　)[1] with a performance by the chorus club. (　　　　)[2], we had originally planned for the school principal to (　　　)[3] a welcome speech. But he prefers that the president (　　　)[4] the student council make the speech, so she (　　　)[5] do that. Instead, the principal will make (　　　)[6] closing address just after the live performance by (　　　)[7] dance team. Finally, a small welcome reception for parents (　　　)[8] be held following the closing address. I think we're (　　　)[9] set for the big day. (　　　)[10] receptionist said the products are grouped by the (　　　)[11] of food, like a supermarket. Sweets are available (　　　)[12] Section C. Dairy or milk-based products are in Section E. We (　　　)[13] get noodles in Section B. That's next to Section A, where (　　　)[14] fruits are located. Drinks are sold in Section D. Oh, and Section F features (　　　)[15] different country each day. Today, items from Greece (　　　)[16] there as well as in (　　　)[17] usual sections.

Tour No. 1 allows you to experience a variety (　　　)[18] contemporary works that well-known artists have produced between the years 2010 (　　　)[19] 2020. It includes both sculptures and paintings. It's self-guided, so you (　　　)[20] go along at your own (　　　)[21], using a detailed guidebook. Tour No. 2, which is available (　　　)[22] this week, focuses on great works (　　　)[23] art of the 21st century. The tour (　　　)[24], who is an art professor at (　　　)[25] local university, will personally guide you through the painting (　　　)²⁶ sculpture exhibits. Tour No. 3 allows you to use a smartphone (　　　)²⁷ listen to a recorded explanation by an art expert. (　　　)²⁸ guide will first cover the painting galleries (　　　)²⁹ then, later, proceed to the ancient sculpture exhibit outdoors. This (　　　)³⁰ great for the independent tourist. In Tour No. 4, (　　　)³¹ guide, who is a local volunteer, (　　　)³² accompany you through a series of exhibits that focus (　　　)³³ paintings from various art periods. It covers works from (　　　)³⁴ 17th century to contemporary times. The sculpture exhibits are not included (　　　)³⁵ this tour.

MET 2022 追（3）日本語訳

問題英文の日本語訳を確認しよう。

親の日のスケジュールを確認してみましょう。イベントは合唱部による演奏で幕開け。次に，当初は校長先生が歓迎の挨拶をすることになってたんだけどね。校長先生は生徒会長がスピーチをした方がいいと思っているのよ。で，生徒会長が，スピーチをする。その代わりに，校長先生が閉会の辞を述べる。ダンスチームによるライブパフォーマンスの直後にね。最後に，保護者向けのささやかな歓迎レセプションが開催される。閉会の辞に続いてね。準備は万端よ。大事な日のね。受付係によると，商品はスーパーマーケットのように食品の種類ごとに分類されているとのこと。お菓子はセクション C で購入できます。乳製品や牛乳ベースの製品はセクション E で購入できます。麺類はセクション B で。セクション B は，セクション A の隣で，セクション A には，果物があります。飲み物は，セクション D で。セクション F では毎日異なる国が紹介されます。本日は，ギリシャからの商品がそこにあります。いつものセクションと同様にね。

ツアー No. 1 では，さまざまな現代作品を体験できます。著名なアーティストが 2010 年から 2020 年にかけて制作した作品。このツアーは，彫刻と絵画の両方を見せてくれます。これは，セルフガイドなので，自分のペースで進むことができます。詳しいガイドブックを手にね。ツアー No. 2 は，今週限定で，21 世紀の偉大な芸術作品に焦点を当てます。ツアーガイドは，地元の大学の美術教授で，絵画や彫刻の展示物を，教授なりのやり方で案内してくれます。ツアー No. 3 では，スマートフォンを使って，美術専門家による録音解説を聞くことができます。ガイドはまず絵画ギャラリーを紹介し，その後，屋外の古代彫刻の展示に進みます。これは個人旅行者にとって最高です。ツアー No. 4 では，ガイドは，地元のボランティアで，一連の展示品を案内してくれます。さまざまな芸術時代の絵画に焦点を当てながら。17 世紀から現代までの作品を網羅しています。彫刻の展示は，このツアーには含まれていません。

MET 2022 追（3）解答

解答付き英文を見ながら，英語の音声をもう一度聞いてみよう。

Let's review the schedule for Parents' Day. The event will (**open**)[1] with a performance by the chorus club. (**Next**)[2], we had originally planned for the school principal to (**make**)[3] a welcome speech. But he prefers that the president (**of**)[4] the student council make the speech, so she (**will**)[5] do that. Instead, the principal will make (**the**)[6] closing address just after the live performance by (**the**)[7] dance team. Finally, a small welcome reception for parents (**will**)[8] be held following the closing address. I think we're (**all**)[9] set for the big day. (**The**)[10] receptionist said the products are grouped by the (**type**)[11] of food, like a supermarket. Sweets are available (**in**)[12] Section C. Dairy or milk-based products are in Section E. We (**can**)[13] get noodles in Section B. That's next to Section A, where (**the**)[14] fruits are located. Drinks are sold in Section D. Oh, and Section F features (**a**)[15] different country each day. Today, items from Greece (**are**)[16] there as well as in (**their**)[17] usual sections.

Tour No. 1 allows you to experience a variety (**of**)[18] contemporary works that well-known artists have produced between the years 2010 (**and**)[19] 2020. It includes both sculptures and paintings. It's self-guided, so you (**can**)[20] go along at your own (**pace**)[21], using a detailed guidebook. Tour No. 2, which is available (**only**)[22] this week, focuses on great works (**of**)[23] art of the 21st century. The tour (**guide**)[24], who is an art professor at (**a**)[25] local university, will personally guide you through the painting (**and**)[26] sculpture exhibits. Tour No. 3 allows you to use a smartphone (**to**)[27] listen to a recorded explanation by an art expert. (**The**)[28] guide will first cover the painting galleries (**and**)[29] then, later, proceed to the ancient sculpture exhibit outdoors. This (**is**)[30] great for the independent tourist. In Tour No. 4, (**the**)[31] guide, who is a local volunteer, (**will**)[32] accompany you through a series of exhibits that focus (**on**)[33] paintings from various art periods. It covers works from (**the**)[34] 17th century to contemporary times. The sculpture exhibits are not included (**in**)[35] this tour.

MET 2022 追 (4)

英語の音声を聞きながら，（　　）の中に，英単語を入れてください。

Our focus today is on (　　　　)[1] tiny animal, the honeybee. Have you ever thought (　　　　)[2] how important they are? By flying from one (　　　　)[3] to another, honeybees pollinate flowers and plants, which is an essential (　　　　)[4] of agricultural crop production worldwide. In fact, almost 35% of (　　　　)[5] global food production relies on honeybees, both wild and domesticated. (　　　　)[6] emphasize the importance of bees, in 2020, the United Nations designated May 20th (　　　　)[7] "World Bee Day." Although honeybees are necessary for human life, they (　　　　)[8] facing serious challenges. Wild honeybees have been at increasing risk (　　　　)[9] extinction. These honeybees and native flowering plants depend on each other (　　　　)[10] survival, but the natural habitats of wild honeybees are (　　　　)[11] destroyed. Factors such as climate change and land development are responsible (　　　　)[12] this loss, leaving these wild honeybees without their natural environments. Domesticated honeybees (　　　　)[13] kept and managed by farmers called beekeepers for the production (　　　　)[14] honey. In recent years, the number of domesticated honeybees (　　　　)[15] been on the decline in many countries. Issues including infectious diseases (　　　　)[16] natural enemies are making it very difficult to sustain beekeeping. How (　　　　)[17] deal with these issues has been (　　　　)[18] concern for beekeepers around the world. What can (　　　　)[19] done to maintain these honeybee populations? For wild honeybees, (　　　　)[20] can grow a variety of bee-friendly plants that (　　　　)[21] in different seasons in order to provide them (　　　　)[22]

healthy habitats. For domesticated honeybees, beekeepers can make use of technological advances ( )^{23} create safer environments that will protect their bees. ( )^{24} improving natural habitats and managing honeybees properly, we can ensure the survival of ( )^{25} only our important friend, the honeybee, but ourselves as ( )^{26}. Now let's focus on honey production. The demand ( )^{27} honey has been growing worldwide, and the United States ( )^{28} one example. Please take a look at the ( )^{29} that shows the top five countries with ( )^{30} highest honey imports between 2008 and 2019. What does this ( )^{31}?

MET 2022 追 (4) 日本語訳

問題英文の日本語訳を確認しよう。

今日私たちが焦点を当てるのは，小さな動物，ミツバチです。ミツバチがどれほど重要であるか考えたことがありますか？ ミツバチは，ある植物から別の植物に飛び回ることで，花や植物に受粉させます。これは世界中の農作物生産に不可欠なものです。実際，世界の食料生産のほぼ 35% は，野生のミツバチと人が飼っているミツバチの両方に依存しています。ミツバチの重要性を強調するために，2020 年に国連は 5 月 20 日を「世界ミツバチの日」と定めました。ミツバチは人間の生活に必要な存在ですが，深刻な問題に直面しています。野生のミツバチは絶滅の危機に瀕しているのです。これらのミツバチと，在来の，花を咲かせて実をならせる植物，顕花植物と言いますが，は生存のために相互に依存しています。しかしながら，野生のミツバチの自然の生息地は破壊されています。気候変動や土地開発などの要因がこの損失の原因で，これらの野生のミツバチは，自然環境を失っています。人が飼っているミツバチは，養蜂家と呼ばれる農家によって飼育・管理されています。蜂蜜を生産するために。近年，多くの国でミツバチの飼育数が減少傾向にあります。感染症や天敵などの問題により，養蜂の継続は非常に困難になっています。これらの問題にどう対処するかは，世界中の養蜂家にとって懸念事項となっています。これらのミツバチの個体数を維持するにはどうすればいいでしょうか？ 野生のミツバチに優しい，さまざまな植物を栽培することができます。さまざまな季節に花を咲かせるような植物です。これは，野生のミツバチにとって健康的な生息地を提供するためです。人が飼っているミツバチの場合，養蜂家は技術の進歩を利用してより安全な環境を作り出すことができます。ミツバチを守るために。自然の生息地を改善し，ミツバチを適切に管理することで，大切な友人であるミツバチだけでなく，私たち自身も生き残ることができます。次に，蜂蜜の生産に焦点を当てましょう。蜂蜜の需要は世界中で高まっており，米国もその一例です。グラフをご覧ください。蜂蜜の輸入量が多かった上位 5 か国のグラフです。2008 年から 2019 年の間に。これは何を意味するのでしょうか？

MET 2022 追（4）解答

解答付き英文を見ながら，英語の音声をもう一度聞いてみよう。

Our focus today is on (**a**)[1] tiny animal, the honeybee. Have you ever thought (**about**)[2] how important they are? By flying from one (**plant**)[3] to another, honeybees pollinate flowers and plants, which is an essential (**part**)[4] of agricultural crop production worldwide. In fact, almost 35% of (**our**)[5] global food production relies on honeybees, both wild and domesticated. (**To**)[6] emphasize the importance of bees, in 2020, the United Nations designated May 20th (**as**)[7] "World Bee Day." Although honeybees are necessary for human life, they (**are**)[8] facing serious challenges. Wild honeybees have been at increasing risk (**of**)[9] extinction. These honeybees and native flowering plants depend on each other (**for**)[10] survival, but the natural habitats of wild honeybees are (**being**)[11] destroyed. Factors such as climate change and land development are responsible (**for**)[12] this loss, leaving these wild honeybees without their natural environments. Domesticated honeybees (**are**)[13] kept and managed by farmers called beekeepers for the production (**of**)[14] honey. In recent years, the number of domesticated honeybees (**has**)[15] been on the decline in many countries. Issues including infectious diseases (**and**)[16] natural enemies are making it very difficult to sustain beekeeping. How (**to**)[17] deal with these issues has been (**a**)[18] concern for beekeepers around the world. What can (**be**)[19] done to maintain these honeybee populations? For wild honeybees, (**we**)[20] can grow a variety of bee-friendly plants that (**bloom**)[21] in different seasons in order to provide them (**with**)[22] healthy habitats. For domesticated honeybees, beekeepers can make use of technological advances (**to**)[23] create safer environments that will protect their bees. (**By**)[24] improving natural habitats and managing honeybees properly, we can ensure the survival of (**not**)[25] only our important friend, the honeybee, but ourselves as (**well**)[26]. Now let's focus on honey production. The demand (**for**)[27] honey has been growing worldwide, and the United States (**is**)[28] one example. Please take a look at the (**graph**)[29] that shows the top five countries with (**the**)[30] highest honey imports between 2008 and 2019. What does this (**imply**)[31]?

英語の音声を聞きながら，（　　）の中に，英単語を入れてください。

How about getting Timmy a violin for his birthday? Oh, (　　　　)¹ you want him to play (　　　　)² an orchestra? I hope he does, eventually. Hmm... (　　　　)³ about a saxophone? It's more fun than (　　　　)⁴ violin. But I want to get (　　　　)⁵ a violin while he's still young. Of course (　　　　)⁶ is important for both instruments. Still, I (　　　　)⁷ hoping that Timmy could play jazz someday. But (　　　　)⁸ the violin, he's stuck with classical music. What's wrong (　　　　)⁹ classical music? Nothing. But what's better about jazz is (　　　　)¹⁰ you can change the melody as you (　　　　)¹¹. There's more freedom. It's more fun. More freedom is (　　　　)¹² very good, but you need (　　　　)¹³ learn to read music first. (　　　　)¹⁴ classical music is the best for (　　　　)¹⁵. Well, Timmy can learn to read music (　　　　)¹⁶ playing jazz on the saxophone. Couldn't he learn (　　　　)¹⁷ saxophone later if he wants? Why don't (　　　　)¹⁸ let him choose? What's important is that he (　　　　)¹⁹ it. Wow, Saki. Look at all your (　　　　)²⁰. Yeah, maybe too many, Joe. I bet (　　　　)²¹ read a lot. Yeah, but I (　　　　)²² read ebooks. They're more portable. Portable? Well, for example, on long (　　　　)²³, you don't have to carry a (　　　　)²⁴ of books with you, right, Keith? That's (　　　　)²⁵, Joe. And not only that, but ebooks (　　　　)²⁶ usually a lot cheaper than paper books. Hmm... ebooks (　　　　)²⁷ sound appealing, but... what do you (　　　　)²⁸, Beth? Do you read ebooks? No. I like looking (　　　　)²⁹ the books I collect on my (　　　　)³⁰. Yeah, Saki's bookcase does look pretty cool. Those books must've (　　　　)³¹ a lot, though. I save money (   )^{32} buying ebooks. That's so economical, Keith. So, how many books (   )^{33} you actually have, Saki? Too many. Storage is (   )^{34} issue for me. Not for (   )^{35}. I've got thousands in my tablet, and it's still (   )^{36} full. I know, Joe. And they probably didn't (   )^{37} very much, right? No, they didn't. Even (   )^{38} my storage problem, I still prefer paper books because (   )^{39} the way they feel. Me, (   )^{40}. Besides, they're easier to study with. In what (   )^{41}, Beth? I feel like I remember more (   )^{42} paper books. And I remember that (   )^{43} have a test tomorrow. I'd better charge up my tablet.

MET 2022 追（5）日本語訳

問題英文の日本語訳を確認しよう。

ティミーの誕生日にバイオリンを買ってやるってのはどうかなあ？ ああ，ティミーにオーケストラで演奏してもらいたいってこと？ 結果的にそうなってくれるといいなと。うーん，サックスはどうかな？ バイオリンよりも楽しいんじゃないかな。でも，私としてはティミーがまだ小さいうちにヴァイオリンを買ってあげたいなと。もちろん，年齢は，どちらの楽器にとっても重要よ。それでも，私としてはティミーがいつかジャズが演奏できたらなって。でも，ヴァイオリンとなると，クラシック音楽が中心にならない？クラシック音楽の何が問題？ いや，そういうわけじゃ。でも，ジャズのいいところは，演奏しながらメロディーを変えることができるってことなのよ。もっと自由があって，もっと楽しい。自由が増えるのはとてもいいことだと思うんだけど，まず楽譜が読めるようになる必要があるよね。で，それにはクラシック音楽が最適だと思うんだ。そうね，ティミーは，楽譜の読み方を学ぶことができると思うのよ。サックスでジャズを演奏しながらでもね。後でサックスを習うことはできないかな？ 本当にやってみたければ。ティミーに選ばせてみない？ 重要なのは，ティミーがそれを楽しむってことだからね。うわー，サキ。あなたの本，全部見てみてよ。そうね，多すぎるかもね，ジョー。ジョーもきっとたくさん読んでるでしょ。うん，でも電子書籍しか読まないんだ。持ち運びに便利だからね。持ち運び？ なんていうか，例えば，旅に出るとしたら，本をたくさん持ち歩く必要がなくなるんだよ，だよね，キース？ そうそう，ジョー。それだけじゃなくって，電子書籍は普通，紙の本よりもうんと安いんだ。うーん，電子書籍は魅力的には聞こえるけど，ベス，どう思う？ 電子書籍を読む方？ いや，私は，どっちかっていうと，本棚に集めた本を見るのが好きなの。そうだね，サキの本棚はなかなかいいもんね。でも，これだけの本，かなりお金かかってるよ。私なら，電子書籍を買ってお金を節約するけどね。キース，そりゃとても経済的。それで，サキは実際何冊本持ってるの？ 大量。収納は，私には大問題。私にはそんな問題起きないよ。タブレットには何千ものデータが入ってるけど，まだいっぱいじゃないし。わかってるよ，ジョー。で，ほとんど費用がかからなかったんでしょ？ そうそう，ほとんど。でも，収納に問題があるとはいえ，私はやっぱり紙の本の方が好きだな。だって触った感触がいいじゃない。私もそう。それに，勉強するとき，便利だし。ベス，どんな具合に？ 紙の本の方が記憶に残るような気がするのよ。で，明日テストがあるよね。タブレット，充電しとこっと。

MET 2022 追（5）解答

解答付き英文を見ながら，英語の音声をもう一度聞いてみよう。

How about getting Timmy a violin for his birthday? Oh, (**do**)[1] you want him to play (**in**)[2] an orchestra? I hope he does, eventually. Hmm... (**how**)[3] about a saxophone? It's more fun than (**the**)[4] violin. But I want to get (**him**)[5] a violin while he's still young. Of course (**age**)[6] is important for both instruments. Still, I (**was**)[7] hoping that Timmy could play jazz someday. But (**with**)[8] the violin, he's stuck with classical music. What's wrong (**with**)[9] classical music? Nothing. But what's better about jazz is (**that**)[10] you can change the melody as you (**play**)[11]. There's more freedom. It's more fun. More freedom is (**all**)[12] very good, but you need (**to**)[13] learn to read music first. (**And**)[14] classical music is the best for (**that**)[15]. Well, Timmy can learn to read music (**while**)[16] playing jazz on the saxophone. Couldn't he learn (**the**)[17] saxophone later if he wants? Why don't (**we**)[18] let him choose? What's important is that he (**enjoy**)[19] it. Wow, Saki. Look at all your (**books**)[20]. Yeah, maybe too many, Joe. I bet (**you**)[21] read a lot. Yeah, but I (**only**)[22] read ebooks. They're more portable. Portable? Well, for example, on long (**trips**)[23], you don't have to carry a (**bunch**)[24] of books with you, right, Keith? That's (**right**)[25], Joe. And not only that, but ebooks (**are**)[26] usually a lot cheaper than paper books. Hmm... ebooks (**do**)[27] sound appealing, but... what do you (**think**)[28], Beth? Do you read ebooks? No. I like looking (**at**)[29] the books I collect on my (**shelf**)[30]. Yeah, Saki's bookcase does look pretty cool. Those books must've (**cost**)[31] a lot, though. I save money (**by**)[32] buying ebooks. That's so economical, Keith. So, how many books (**do**)[33] you actually have, Saki? Too many. Storage is (**an**)[34] issue for me. Not for (**me**)[35]. I've got thousands in my tablet, and it's still (**not**)[36] full. I know, Joe. And they probably didn't (**cost**)[37] very much, right? No, they didn't. Even (**with**)[38] my storage problem, I still prefer paper books because (**of**)[39] the way they feel. Me, (**too**)[40]. Besides, they're easier to study with. In what (**way**)[41], Beth? I feel like I remember more (**with**)[42] paper books. And I remember that (**we**)[43] have a test tomorrow. I'd better charge up my tablet.

MET 2023 追 (1)

英語の音声を聞きながら，（　　　）の中に，英単語を入れてください。

What a beautiful sweater! It looks really (　　　　)[1] on you, Jennifer.
Bowling is more (　　　　)[2] than badminton, but tennis is the (　　　　)[3].
Let's play that. We should go somewhere (　　　　)[4] eat dinner. How
about a (　　　　)[5] restaurant? Diana, do you know what (　　　　)[6] the
dentist will open? My (　　　　)[7] really hurts. The guitar is inside the
(　　　　)[8] under the table. These spoons (　　　　)[9] dirty, but there's another in the drawer. (　　　　)[10] left at the tree (　　　　)[11] go straight.
The apartment building will be (　　　　)[12] the right. Fireflies hatch from
(　　　　)[13]. And in the next (　　　　)[14], they live underwater. I know
(　　　　)[15]. But then, they continue developing underground? Yes.
Didn't you (　　　　)[16] that? No. Aren't fireflies amazing? Which stage
has (　　　　)[17] man just learned about? We (　　　　)[18] to make twenty
eco-friendly bags, so (　　　　)[19] simple design is best. Is a pocket necessary? Definitely, (　　　　)[20] we don't have enough time to (　　　　)[21]
buttons. So, this design! Which eco-friendly bag (　　　　)[22] they make?
I'm here. Wow, there (　　　　)[23] so many different tents. Which one's
(　　　　)[24]? Mine's round. Can't you see it? No. (　　　　)[25] is it? It's
between the trees. (　　　　)[26] one is the brother's tent? We (　　　　)[27]
take the ferry to (　　　　)[28] garden, then the aquarium. I want
(　　　　)[29] visit the shrine, too. But, don't forget, dinner (　　　　)[30] at
six. OK. Let's go there tomorrow. Which (　　　　)[31] will they take
today?

MET 2023 追 (1) 日本語訳

問題英文の日本語訳を確認しよう。

なんてきれいなセーター！ ジェニファー，よく似合ってるよ。ボーリングはバドミントンより楽しいけど，やっぱりテニスが一番だ。テニスしよう。夕食にどこかに行かなきゃね。ステーキレストランはどう？ ダイアナ，歯医者は何時に開くか知ってる？ 歯がまじで痛いの。そのギターはテーブルの下のケースの中にある。このスプーンは汚れているが，引き出しの中に別のスプーンがある。その木のところで左折して，そして，直進してください。右手にマンションがあります。ホタルは卵から孵化する。そして次の段階になると，水中で生活する。そんなこと知ってるわよ。でも，その後，ホタルは地下で大きくなるの？ そう。知らなかった？ 知らなかったよ。ホタルってすごくない？ この男性は，ホタルのどの段階について今学びましたか？ エコバッグを 20 枚作る必要があるの。だから，シンプルなデザインがベストじゃないかなって。ポケットは必要？ 絶対。でも，ボタンを付けてる時間がないのよ。じゃあ，このデザインね！ どのエコバッグを作ってくれるでしょうか？ 私はここよ。うわー，いろんなテントがあるのね。どれがあなたの？ 私のは丸いの。見えない？ 見えないなあ。どこ？ 木と木の間にあるよ。どれが兄のテントですか？ フェリーに乗って庭園に行き，そこから水族館に行けるよ。私は，神社にも行きたいな。でも，忘れないでね，夕食は 6 時。了解。じゃあ，明日そこに行こう。彼らは今日どのルートを通るでしょうか？

MET 2023 追（1）解答

解答付き英文を見ながら，英語の音声をもう一度聞いてみよう。

What a beautiful sweater! It looks really (**nice**)[1] on you, Jennifer. Bowling is more (**fun**)[2] than badminton, but tennis is the (**best**)[3]. Let's play that. We should go somewhere (**to**)[4] eat dinner. How about a (**steak**)[5] restaurant? Diana, do you know what (**time**)[6] the dentist will open? My (**tooth**)[7] really hurts. The guitar is inside the (**case**)[8] under the table. These spoons (**are**)[9] dirty, but there's another in the drawer. (**Turn**)[10] left at the tree (**and**)[11] go straight. The apartment building will be (**on**)[12] the right. Fireflies hatch from (**eggs**)[13]. And in the next (**stage**)[14], they live underwater. I know (**that**)[15]. But then, they continue developing underground? Yes. Didn't you (**know**)[16] that? No. Aren't fireflies amazing? Which stage has (**the**)[17] man just learned about? We (**need**)[18] to make twenty eco-friendly bags, so (**a**)[19] simple design is best. Is a pocket necessary? Definitely, (**but**)[20] we don't have enough time to (**add**)[21] buttons. So, this design! Which eco-friendly bag (**will**)[22] they make? I'm here. Wow, there (**are**)[23] so many different tents. Which one's (**yours**)[24]? Mine's round. Can't you see it? No. (**Where**)[25] is it? It's between the trees. (**Which**)[26] one is the brother's tent? We (**can**)[27] take the ferry to (**the**)[28] garden, then the aquarium. I want (**to**)[29] visit the shrine, too. But, don't forget, dinner (**is**)[30] at six. OK. Let's go there tomorrow. Which (**route**)[31] will they take today?

MET 2023 追（2）

／42 点

英語の音声を聞きながら，（　　）の中に，英単語を入れてください。

Are you going somewhere this summer? Yes, I'm (　　　　)¹ to drive to the (　　　　)². That's quite far. Why don't you (　　　　)³ the train, instead? If I (　　　　)⁴, I can park and (　　　　)⁵ sightseeing anywhere along the way. Isn't driving more expensive? Well, (　　　　)⁶, but I like the flexibility. (　　　　)⁷ much does it cost (　　　　)⁸ send this letter to London? Hmm. Let (　　　　)⁹ check. That's about ₤2 for standard delivery, or (　　　　)¹⁰ ₤8 for special delivery. Which do you prefer? (　　　　)¹¹ really want it to arrive by Friday. (　　　　)¹² special delivery, it will. I'll do that (　　　　)¹³. Would you like to (　　　　)¹⁴ a movie next week? (　　　　)¹⁵, but what kind of (　　　　)¹⁶? I'd like to watch a horror (　　　　)¹⁷. Well, I don't see one scheduled, but there's a comedy currently showing. (　　　　)¹⁸ really don't like comedies. Maybe we can (　　　　)¹⁹ the schedule again next week. (　　　　)²⁰, let's do that. What did (　　　　)²¹ do last weekend? I took (　　　　)²² my nieces and nephews to lunch. Really? (　　　　)²³ many do you have? Well, (　　　　)²⁴ sister has two boys, and my brother (　　　　)²⁵ three girls. That sounds like a (　　　　)²⁶ family gathering. Yes, we had a really good (　　　　)²⁷ together. I think I'll have the (　　　　)²⁸. The fish looks nice. I'll (　　　　)²⁹ that. What about for dessert? (　　　　)³⁰ the pie and the (　　　　)³¹ look delicious. Well, why don't we each (　　　　)³² different ones? Then we can (　　　　)³³. OK, I'll order the pie and (　　　　)³⁴ can order the cake. (　　　　)³⁵, that's fine. Hi, Monica, would you like (　　　　)³⁶ help? Ah, thank you. Could (　　　　)³⁷ take one of these bags? (　　　　)³⁸, are you going to (　　　　)³⁹ subway? No, I'm going to take them (　　　　)⁴⁰ in my car. I've parked just around (　　　　)⁴¹ corner. That's fine. Actually, it's on my way. That's (　　　　)⁴² before my bus stop.

MET 2023 追 (2) 日本語訳

問題英文の日本語訳を確認しよう。

今年の夏はどこかに行くの？ ええ，海岸まで車で行こうかなと。けっこうな距離だよね。代わりに電車で行くってのは？ 車なら，途中でどこにでも駐車して観光できるからねえ。車を運転した方が高くつかない？ まあ，そうかも知れないけど，車はなにかと自由がきくからね。いくらかかりますか，この手紙をロンドンに送ると？ えーっと，確認しますね。普通郵便の場合は約2ポンド，速達の場合は約8ポンドですね。どちらにしましょうか？ 金曜日までには届いて欲しいんですよね。速達なら，大丈夫です。じゃあ，速達で。来週映画を見ない？ いいけど，どんな映画？ ホラー映画が見たいんだけど。そうだねえ，上映予定がないみたいだよ。今は，コメディが上映されてる。コメディがあまり好きじゃないんだよねえ。来週またスケジュール確認しようか。そうだね，そうしよう。先週末は，何したの？ 私は姪と甥を全員昼食に連れてったよ。本当に？ 何人？ 妹のところは，男の子が2人，兄のところは，女の子が3人。いい感じの家族の集まりだね。そう，本当に楽しかったよ。パスタを食べようかな。魚もいい感じ。私は魚にしよう。デザートは何にする？ パイもケーキも美味しそう。じゃあ，それぞれ違うのを注文しない？ そうすればシェアできる。いいね。じゃあ，私がパイを注文するので，ケーキを注文してね。了解。いいね。こんにちは，モニカ，助けが必要？ ああ，ありがとう。このバッグを1つ持ってもらえる？ いいよ，地下鉄に行くの？ いえ，車に積んで，家まで帰ろうと。すぐ角を曲がったところに駐車してあるの。そりゃいいや。実は，私もちょうどそっちに行くところだったのよ。乗ろうと思ってるバス停の直前なのよ。

MET 2023 追（2）解答

解答付き英文を見ながら，英語の音声をもう一度聞いてみよう。

Are you going somewhere this summer? Yes, I'm（ **going** ）[1] to drive to the（ **coast** ）[2]. That's quite far. Why don't you（ **take** ）[3] the train, instead? If I（ **drive** ）[4], I can park and（ **go** ）[5] sightseeing anywhere along the way. Isn't driving more expensive? Well,（ **maybe** ）[6], but I like the flexibility. （ **How** ）[7] much does it cost（ **to** ）[8] send this letter to London? Hmm. Let（ **me** ）[9] check. That's about ₤2 for standard delivery, or（ **about** ）[10] ₤8 for special delivery. Which do you prefer? （ **I** ）[11] really want it to arrive by Friday. （ **With** ）[12] special delivery, it will. I'll do that（ **then** ）[13]. Would you like to（ **see** ）[14] a movie next week? （ **Sure** ）[15], but what kind of（ **movie** ）[16]? I'd like to watch a horror（ **movie** ）[17]. Well, I don't see one scheduled, but there's a comedy currently showing. （ **I** ）[18] really don't like comedies. Maybe we can（ **check** ）[19] the schedule again next week. （ **Sure** ）[20], let's do that. What did（ **you** ）[21] do last weekend? I took（ **all** ）[22] my nieces and nephews to lunch. Really? （ **How** ）[23] many do you have? Well,（ **my** ）[24] sister has two boys, and my brother（ **has** ）[25] three girls. That sounds like a（ **nice** ）[26] family gathering. Yes, we had a really good（ **time** ）[27] together. I think I'll have the（ **pasta** ）[28]. The fish looks nice. I'll（ **order** ）[29] that. What about for dessert? （ **Both** ）[30] the pie and the（ **cake** ）[31] look delicious. Well, why don't we each（ **order** ）[32] different ones? Then we can（ **share** ）[33]. OK, I'll order the pie and（ **you** ）[34] can order the cake. （ **Sure** ）[35], that's fine. Hi, Monica, would you like（ **some** ）[36] help? Ah, thank you. Could（ **you** ）[37] take one of these bags? （ **Sure** ）[38], are you going to（ **the** ）[39] subway? No, I'm going to take them（ **home** ）[40] in my car. I've parked just around（ **the** ）[41] corner. That's fine. Actually, it's on my way. That's（ **just** ）[42] before my bus stop.

MET 2023 追 (3)

英語の音声を聞きながら，（　　）の中に，英単語を入れてください。

To understand our campus services, we researched the number (　　　　)[1] students who used the cafeteria, computer room, library, (　　　　)[2] student lounge over the last semester. As (　　　　)[3] can see, the student lounge had (　　　　)[4] continuous rise in users over (　　　　)[5] four months. The use of the computer (　　　　)[6], however, was the least consistent, with (　　　　)[7] increase and some decrease. Library usage dropped in May (　　　　)[8] grew each month after (　　　　)[9]. Finally, cafeteria use rose in May, and (　　　　)[10] the numbers became stable. Let me explain our monthly membership (　　　　)[11]. A regular membership with 24-hour access to all (　　　　)[12] is ¥8,000. Daytime members can access all areas (　　　　)[13] ¥5,000. Students with a valid ID get half-off (　　　　)[14] regular membership fee. We also offer pool-only options (　　　　)[15] ¥2,000 off the price of (　　　　)[16] regular, daytime, and student memberships. Oh, and our towel service (　　　　)[17] included in our regular membership with no (　　　　)[18] charge but is available to daytime and student members (　　　　)[19] an additional ¥1,000.

I suggest the Ashford Center. It (　　　　)[20] twenty rooms we can use (　　　　)[21] sessions that hold up to forty people (　　　　)[22] and a conference room for meetings. It's recently (　　　　)[23] updated with Wi-Fi available everywhere, and it has (　　　　)[24] excellent food court. I recommend the Founders' Hotel. It's modern (　　　　)[25] Wi-Fi in all rooms, and (　　　　)[26] great restaurants are available just a five-minute

(   )^{27} from the building. They have plenty (   )^{28} space for lectures with eight large (   )^{29} that accommodate seventy people each. I like Mountain Terrace. (   )^{30} course, there are several restaurants inside for people to choose (   )^{31}, and Wi-Fi is available throughout the hotel. (   )^{32} have ten rooms that can (   )^{33} sixty people each, but unfortunately they don't have (   )^{34} printing service. Valley Hall is great! They have (   )^{35} of space with five huge (   )^{36} that fit up to 200 people (   )^{37}. There's a restaurant on the top (   )^{38} with a fantastic view of (   )^{39} mountains. If you need Wi-Fi, it's available in (   )^{40} lobby.

MET 2023 追 (3) 日本語訳

問題英文の日本語訳を確認しよう。

キャンパスサービスを理解するために，私たちは，学生の数を調査しました。前の学期に，カフェテリア，コンピュータルーム，図書館，学生ラウンジを利用した学生の数。ご覧のとおり，学生ラウンジは4か月間を通じて利用者数が増加し続けています。しかし，コンピューター室の使用量は最も一貫性がなく，多少の増加と若干の減少が見られました。図書館の利用は5月に減少しましたが，その後毎月増加しました。最後に，5月にカフェテリアの利用が増加し，その後，数字は安定しました。月額会員プランについてご説明いたします。通常会員は，24時間全エリア利用可能で，8,000円。デイタイム会員は5,000円で全エリアご利用いただけます。学生は，有効な身分証明書をお持ちの場合は，通常会費の半額になります。プールのみのオプションは，通常会員，デイタイム会員，学生会員より2,000円引きで，ご用意しております。それと，タオルサービスは通常会員は無料ですが，デイタイム会員と学生会員は1,000円増しでご利用いただけます。

アッシュフォードセンターをお勧めします。20室は，それぞれ40人まで収容できるセッションに使用でき，また，ミーティング用の会議室もあります。最近改装され，どこでもWi-Fiが利用できるようになり，素晴らしいフードコートもあります。ファウンダーズホテルをお勧めします。全室Wi-Fi完備のモダンなホテルで，建物から徒歩わずか5分のところに素晴らしいレストランがたくさんあります。講義用の十分なスペースがあり，大きな部屋が8つあり，それぞれ70人収容できます。マウンテンテラスがいいと思います。もちろん，館内にはいくつかのレストランがあり，ホテル全体でWi-Fiが利用可能です。10部屋あり，それぞれ60人収容できますが，残念ながら印刷サービスはありません。バレーホールがいいと思います！ 広々としたスペースがあります。大きな部屋が5つあり，それぞれ200人まで収容できます。最上階にはレストランがあり，山々の素晴らしい眺めが楽しめます。Wi-Fiが必要な場合は，ロビーでご利用いただけます。

MET 2023 追（3）解答

解答付き英文を見ながら，英語の音声をもう一度聞いてみよう。

To understand our campus services, we researched the number (**of**)[1] students who used the cafeteria, computer room, library, (**and**)[2] student lounge over the last semester. As (**you**)[3] can see, the student lounge had (**a**)[4] continuous rise in users over (**all**)[5] four months. The use of the computer (**room**)[6], however, was the least consistent, with (**some**)[7] increase and some decrease. Library usage dropped in May (**but**)[8] grew each month after (**that**)[9]. Finally, cafeteria use rose in May, and (**then**)[10] the numbers became stable. Let me explain our monthly membership (**plans**)[11]. A regular membership with 24-hour access to all (**areas**)[12] is ¥8,000. Daytime members can access all areas (**for**)[13] ¥5,000. Students with a valid ID get half-off (**our**)[14] regular membership fee. We also offer pool-only options (**for**)[15] ¥2,000 off the price of (**our**)[16] regular, daytime, and student memberships. Oh, and our towel service (**is**)[17] included in our regular membership with no (**extra**)[18] charge but is available to daytime and student members (**for**)[19] an additional ¥1,000.

I suggest the Ashford Center. It (**has**)[20] twenty rooms we can use (**for**)[21] sessions that hold up to forty people (**each**)[22] and a conference room for meetings. It's recently (**been**)[23] updated with Wi-Fi available everywhere, and it has (**an**)[24] excellent food court. I recommend the Founders' Hotel. It's modern (**with**)[25] Wi-Fi in all rooms, and (**many**)[26] great restaurants are available just a five-minute (**walk**)[27] from the building. They have plenty (**of**)[28] space for lectures with eight large (**rooms**)[29] that accommodate seventy people each. I like Mountain Terrace. (**Of**)[30] course, there are several restaurants inside for people to choose (**from**)[31], and Wi-Fi is available throughout the hotel. (**They**)[32] have ten rooms that can (**hold**)[33] sixty people each, but unfortunately they don't have (**a**)[34] printing service. Valley Hall is great! They have (**lots**)[35] of space with five huge (**rooms**)[36] that fit up to 200 people (**each**)[37]. There's a restaurant on the top (**floor**)[38] with a fantastic view of (**the**)[39] mountains. If you need Wi-Fi, it's available in (**the**)[40] lobby.

MET 2023 追 (4)

英語の音声を聞きながら，（　　）の中に，英単語を入れてください。

Today, we're going to focus (　　　　　)[1] art in the digital age. (　　　　)[2] advances in technology, how people view art (　　　　)[3] changing. In recent years, some art collections (　　　　)[4] been put online to create "digital art museums." Why (　　　　)[5] art museums moving to digital spaces? One reason has to (　　　　)[6] with visitor access. In digital museums, visitors can experience art without (　　　　)[7] limitation of physical spaces. If museums are online, more people (　　　　)[8] make virtual visits to them. Also, (　　　　)[9] online museums never close, visitors can stay (　　　　)[10] as long as they (　　　　)[11]! Another reason is related to how collections are displayed. Online exhibits enable visitors (　　　　)[12] watch videos, see the artwork from various angles, (　　　　)[13] use interactive features. This gives visitors much (　　　　)[14] specific information about each collection. Putting collections online takes extra effort, (　　　　)[15], and money. First, museum directors must (　　　　)[16] eager to try this (　　　　)[17] format. Then, they have to (　　　　)[18] the time to hire specialists (　　　　)[19] raise the money to (　　　　)[20] the necessary technology. Of course, many people might (　　　　)[21] want to see the actual pieces themselves. (　　　　)[22] factors are some reasons why not (　　　　)[23] museums are adding an online format. Many art museums (　　　　)[24] been offering digital versions of their museums for (　　　　)[25], but this system might change in (　　　　)[26] future. Museums will probably need to depend on income (　　　　)[27] a hybrid style of both in-person (　　　　)[28] online visitors. This kind of income could enable（　　　　）²⁹ to remain financially sustainable for future generations. Now, let's do（　　　　）³⁰ presentations.　Group 1, start when you （　　　　）³¹ ready.　Our group looked at（　　　　）³² survey of 56 art museums conducted in the（　　　　）³³ of 2020.　Many art museums are currently thinking（　　　　）³⁴ how to go digital.　This survey specifically （　　　　）³⁵ if art museums were putting their exhibition videos （　　　　）³⁶ the internet.　Here are those survey results.

MET 2023 追（4）日本語訳

問題英文の日本語訳を確認しよう。

今日はデジタル時代のアートに焦点を当てます。テクノロジーの進歩により，人々のアートに対する見方も変わりつつあります。近年，一部の美術コレクションがオンライン上で公開され，「デジタル美術館」が開設されています。なぜ美術館はデジタル空間に移行するのでしょうか？ その理由の1つは訪問者のアクセスに関係しています。デジタルミュージアムでは，物理的な空間に制限されずにアートが体験できます。美術館がオンライン化すれば，より多くの人が仮想訪問できるようになります。また，オンライン美術館は閉館することがないので，好きなだけ滞在できます。もう1つの理由は，コレクションの展示方法に関連しています。オンライン展示では，訪問者は，ビデオを視聴したり，さまざまな角度から作品を鑑賞したり，対話式の機能を使用したりできます。これにより，訪問者は各コレクションに関して，より具体的な情報を得ることができます。コレクションをオンライン公開するには，これまで以上の労力，時間，費用がかかります。まず，博物館の館長は，この新しい形式を試してみたいと思っていなければいけません。次に，専門家を雇い，資金を調達する必要があります。必要なテクノロジーを購入するために。もちろん，実際に作品を見てみたいという人も多くいるかもしれません。これらの要因があるため，必ずしもすべての美術館がオンライン形式を追加していないのです。多くの美術館がそのデジタル版を無料で提供してきていますが，この制度は将来的に変わる可能性があります。美術館はおそらく，次のような収入に依存する必要があるでしょう。それは，対面とオンラインの両方の訪問者からのハイブリッド型収入です。この種の収入により，将来の世代に向けて，経済的に持続可能な状態を維持できる可能性があります。それでは，プレゼンテーションを行いますね。グループ1，準備ができたら開始してください。私たちのグループは，2020年の秋に56の美術館を対象に実施した調査結果を見てみました。現在，デジタル化を検討している美術館がたくさんあります。この調査では，美術館が展示ビデオをインターネット上に公開しているかどうかについて，限定して尋ねました。こちらがその調査結果です。

MET 2023 追（4）解答

解答付き英文を見ながら，英語の音声をもう一度聞いてみよう。

Today, we're going to focus (**on**)¹ art in the digital age. (**With**)² advances in technology, how people view art (**is**)³ changing. In recent years, some art collections (**have**)⁴ been put online to create "digital art museums." Why (**are**)⁵ art museums moving to digital spaces? One reason has to (**do**)⁶ with visitor access. In digital museums, visitors can experience art without (**the**)⁷ limitation of physical spaces. If museums are online, more people (**can**)⁸ make virtual visits to them. Also, (**as**)⁹ online museums never close, visitors can stay (**for**)¹⁰ as long as they (**like**)¹¹! Another reason is related to how collections are displayed. Online exhibits enable visitors (**to**)¹² watch videos, see the artwork from various angles, (**and**)¹³ use interactive features. This gives visitors much (**more**)¹⁴ specific information about each collection. Putting collections online takes extra effort, (**time**)¹⁵, and money. First, museum directors must (**be**)¹⁶ eager to try this (**new**)¹⁷ format. Then, they have to (**take**)¹⁸ the time to hire specialists (**and**)¹⁹ raise the money to (**buy**)²⁰ the necessary technology. Of course, many people might (**still**)²¹ want to see the actual pieces themselves. (**These**)²² factors are some reasons why not (**all**)²³ museums are adding an online format. Many art museums (**have**)²⁴ been offering digital versions of their museums for (**free**)²⁵, but this system might change in (**the**)²⁶ future. Museums will probably need to depend on income (**from**)²⁷ a hybrid style of both in-person (**and**)²⁸ online visitors. This kind of income could enable (**them**)²⁹ to remain financially sustainable for future generations. Now, let's do (**our**)³⁰ presentations. Group 1, start when you (**are**)³¹ ready. Our group looked at (**a**)³² survey of 56 art museums conducted in the (**fall**)³³ of 2020. Many art museums are currently thinking (**about**)³⁴ how to go digital. This survey specifically (**asked**)³⁵ if art museums were putting their exhibition videos (**on**)³⁶ the internet. Here are those survey results.

英語の音声を聞きながら，（　　）の中に，英単語を入れてください。

Our trip is getting close, Mana! Yes, (　　　)^1 need to buy a (　　　)^2 bag to protect my camera and lenses. Aren't (　　　)^3 heavy? I'm just going to (　　　)^4 my smartphone to take pictures. With smartphone software (　　　)^5 can edit your photos quickly and easily. Yeah, (　　)^6 guess so. Then, why (　　)^7 you want to bring (　　)^8 camera and lenses? Because I'm planning to take pictures at (　　)^9 wildlife park. I want my equipment (　　　)^{10} capture detailed images of the animals there. I (　　　)^{11}. Then, I'll take pictures of us having (　　　)^{12} good time, and you photograph (　　　)^{13} animals. Sure! I have three lenses for different purposes. That's (　　　)^{14} to be a lot (　　　)^{15} stuff. I hate carrying heavy luggage. (　　　)^{16} do, too, but since (　　　)^{17} need my camera and lenses, I (　　　)^{18} no choice. I think it'll be (　　　)^{19} it, though. I'm sure it will. I'm looking forward (　　　)^{20} seeing your pictures! Thanks. So, Sally, we have (　　　)^{21} start thinking about graduation research. I know, Jeff. (　　　)^{22} we can choose to work together (　　　)^{23} a group or do (　　　)^{24} individually. I'm leaning towards the group project. What do (　　　)^{25} think, Matt? Well, Jeff, I'm attracted to the idea (　　　)^{26} doing it on my (　　　)^{27}. I've never attempted anything like that before. I (　　　)^{28} to try it. How (　　　)^{29} you, Sally? Same for me, Matt. (　　　)^{30} want to really deepen my understanding of (　　　)^{31} research topic. Besides, I can get one-on-one (　　　)^{32} from a professor. Which do (　　　)^{33} prefer, Aki? I prefer group work because I'd like

(   )[34] develop my communication skills in order to (   )[35] a good leader in the future. (   )[36]. Coming from Japan, you can bring (   )[37] great perspective to a group project. I'd (   )[38] to work with you, Aki. Matt, don't (   )[39] think it'd be better to collaborate? Yes, it (   )[40] sound fun, Jeff. Come to (   )[41] of it, I can (   )[42] from other students if I'm in (   )[43] group. We can work (   )[44] it together. Would you like (   )[45] join us, Sally? Sorry. It's better if (   )[46] do my own research because I'm interested in graduate school. Oh, (   )[47] bad. Well, for our group project, (   )[48] shall we do first? Let's choose (   )[49] group leader. Any volunteers? I'll do it! Fantastic, Aki!

MET 2023 追 (5) 日本語訳

問題英文の日本語訳を確認しよう。

マナ，旅はもうすぐそこよ！ そうそう，新しいバッグを買わなきゃ。カメラとレンズを保護しなくちゃ。重くない？ 私なら，スマホを使って写真を撮るだけなんだけど。スマホのソフトを使えば，写真をすばやく簡単に編集できるし。そりゃそうだね。じゃあ，なんでまた，カメラやレンズを持ってくの？ 野生動物公園で写真を撮りたいの。自分のカメラで，そこにいる動物の詳細な姿をとらえたいのよ。なるほど。じゃあ，こうしない？ 私が人の写真，つまり，楽しい時間を過ごしている写真を撮って，マナは動物の写真を撮る。もちろん！ 用途に合わせて3つのレンズを持っていくわ。けっこうな荷物だね。私は，重い荷物を持つのが好きじゃないんだなあ。私もそうだけど，カメラとレンズが必要なので仕方ないよ。でもそれだけの価値はあると思う。きっとそうだ。マナの写真を見るのが楽しみ！ ありがとう。じゃあ，サリー，そろそろ卒業研究について考え始めないとね。そうね，ジェフ。グループとして一緒に作業するか，個別に作業するか選べるんだけど。私はグループプロジェクトに一票かな。マット，どう思う？ そうだねえ，ジェフ，私は自分でやるという方に一票かなあ。これまで一人でやるなんてこと，なかったから。試してみたいな。サリーは，どう？ マット，私も同じかな。研究テーマについてしっかりと理解を深めたいと思ってるの。それに，教授からマンツーマンで指導を受けることもできるし。アキは，どっちがいいの？ 私は，グループワークに一票。だって，コミュニケーションスキルを磨いて，将来いいリーダーになりたいから。いいね。日本から来てるから，アキは，グループプロジェクトに素晴らしい視点を与えてくれるんじゃないかな。私は，アキと一緒にやりたいな。マット，コラボしたほうがいいと思わない？ そうだね，楽しそうだ，ジェフ。考えてみれば，他の生徒からも学べるしね，グループに属してたら。一緒に取り組めるよね。サリー，一緒にやらない？ ごめん。私，自分で研究した方がいいと思うの。だって，大学院に興味があるから。あら，困った。じゃあ，グループプロジェクトでは，最初に何をしようか？ まず，グループリーダーを決めようよ。やりたい人，いる？ 私，やる！ アキ，素晴らしい！

MET 2023 追 (5) 解答

解答付き英文を見ながら，英語の音声をもう一度聞いてみよう。

Our trip is getting close, Mana! Yes, (**I**)[1] need to buy a (**new**)[2] bag to protect my camera and lenses. Aren't (**they**)[3] heavy? I'm just going to (**use**)[4] my smartphone to take pictures. With smartphone software (**you**)[5] can edit your photos quickly and easily. Yeah, (**I**)[6] guess so. Then, why (**do**)[7] you want to bring (**your**)[8] camera and lenses? Because I'm planning to take pictures at (**the**)[9] wildlife park. I want my equipment (**to**)[10] capture detailed images of the animals there. I (**see**)[11]. Then, I'll take pictures of us having (**a**)[12] good time, and you photograph (**the**)[13] animals. Sure! I have three lenses for different purposes. That's (**going**)[14] to be a lot (**of**)[15] stuff. I hate carrying heavy luggage. (**I**)[16] do, too, but since (**I**)[17] need my camera and lenses, I (**have**)[18] no choice. I think it'll be (**worth**)[19] it, though. I'm sure it will. I'm looking forward (**to**)[20] seeing your pictures! Thanks. So, Sally, we have (**to**)[21] start thinking about graduation research. I know, Jeff. (**And**)[22] we can choose to work together (**as**)[23] a group or do (**it**)[24] individually. I'm leaning towards the group project. What do (**you**)[25] think, Matt? Well, Jeff, I'm attracted to the idea (**of**)[26] doing it on my (**own**)[27]. I've never attempted anything like that before. I (**want**)[28] to try it. How (**about**)[29] you, Sally? Same for me, Matt. (**I**)[30] want to really deepen my understanding of (**the**)[31] research topic. Besides, I can get one-on-one (**help**)[32] from a professor. Which do (**you**)[33] prefer, Aki? I prefer group work because I'd like (**to**)[34] develop my communication skills in order to (**be**)[35] a good leader in the future. (**Cool**)[36]. Coming from Japan, you can bring (**a**)[37] great perspective to a group project. I'd (**love**)[38] to work with you, Aki. Matt, don't (**you**)[39] think it'd be better to collaborate? Yes, it (**does**)[40] sound fun, Jeff. Come to (**think**)[41] of it, I can (**learn**)[42] from other students if I'm in (**a**)[43] group. We can work (**on**)[44] it together. Would you like (**to**)[45] join us, Sally? Sorry. It's better if (**I**)[46] do my own research because I'm interested in graduate school. Oh, (**too**)[47] bad. Well, for our group project, (**what**)[48] shall we do first? Let's choose (**the**)[49] group leader. Any volunteers? I'll do it! Fantastic, Aki!

牧　秀樹（まき　ひでき）

　岐阜大学地域科学部シニア教授。1995 年にコネチカット大学にて博士号（言語学）を取得。研究対象は，言語学と英語教育。

　主な著書：*Essays on Irish Syntax*（共著，2011 年），*Essays on Mongolian Syntax*（共著，2015 年），*Essays on Irish Syntax II*（共著，2017 年），『The Minimal English Test（最小英語テスト）研究』（2018 年），『誰でも言語学』，『最小英語テスト（MET）ドリル』〈標準レベル：高校生から社会人〉，〈センター試験レベル〉，『中学生版 最小英語テスト（jMET）ドリル』（以上，2019 年），「英語 monogrammar シリーズ」『関係詞』『比較』『準動詞』『助動詞・仮定法』『時制・相』『動詞』（監修，以上，2020-2021 年），『金言版 最小英語テスト（kMET）ドリル』（2020 年），『これでも言語学—中国の中の「日本語」』，*Essays on Case*（以上，2021 年），『それでも言語学—ヒトの言葉の意外な約束』，『最小日本語テスト（MJT）ドリル』，『最小中国語テスト（MCT）ドリル』，『最小韓国語テスト（MKT）ドリル』（以上，2022 年），『MCT 中国語実践会話—学びなおしとステップアップ 上海出張・日本紹介』（共著，2023 年），『象の鼻から言語学—主語・目的語カメレオン説』（2023 年），『みんなの言語学入門—日本語と英語の仕組みから未知の言語へ』，『火星人とはなしたよ—地球人のことばは，ほとんどおなじなんだって』（2023 年）［以上，開拓社］，『10 分でわかる！ことばの仕組み』（2023 年，Kindle Direct Publishing），『最小英語テスト（MET）ドリル〈大学入学共通テスト読解版〉』（2024 年，開拓社）など。

張　超（ちょう　ちょう）

　岐阜大学大学院地域科学研究科在学中。牧秀樹研究室に所属。研究対象は，最小日本語テスト。

最小英語テスト（MET）ドリル
〈大学入学共通テスト聴解版〉

ISBN978-4-7589-2338-5　C0082

著作者	牧　秀樹・張　超	
発行者	武村哲司	
印刷所	日之出印刷株式会社	

2024 年 6 月 12 日　第 1 版第 1 刷発行Ⓒ

発行所　　株式会社　開拓社

〒112-0013　東京都文京区音羽 1-22-16
電話　（03）5395-7101（代表）
振替　00160-8-39587
https://www.kaitakusha.co.jp